INDIAN CLOTHING OF THE GREAT LAKES: 1740-1840

REVISED EDITION

BY
SHERYL HARTMAN
WITH ILLUSTRATIONS BY
GREG HUDSON, JOE LEE
AND RALPH HEATH

Eagle's View Publishing Company
6756 North Fork Road
Liberty, UT 84310

Library of Congress Catalog Card Number: 87-83307
ISBN 0-943604-16-8

FIRST REVISED EDITION

10 9 8 7 6 5 4 3 2 1

TABLE OF CONTENTS

PREFACE

Tribal identification of clothing is not as important as the general appearance of the Indians in the area in a particular time period. Styles and designs were shared whether intentionally or by parallel development. This is due in part because of the European trade wars. Goods of similar value being distributed throughout the regions of the eastern half of the states created a strong regional style rather than independent tribal fashions. Tribal Confederacies were strong in the French & Indian War Period as well as the Revolutionary War Period. Thus not only political ties were established by united tribes but also the way in which European goods were utilized to a great extent.

However, there were variations with distinct political groups. The Iroquois tended to develop more distinctive bead applique designs and the Great Lakes tribes tended more towards the development of silk ribbon applique. They preferred using the beads as a continued form of edging a garment and interweaving them with wool yarn in bags and sashes.

Many of the styles and designs indicated in the drawings by Greg Hudson and Joe Lee were taken from original examples and put into use as part of complete ensembles. Many of the patterns for making these garments are included in this book, but often are general in sizes given. This is due in part to the fact that the clothing needs to be fitted to individual measurements, especially for such things as wrap-around skirts and leggings. Shirts and blanket coats are usually large and "blousy" and one size tends to fit persons of varying sizes.

SPECIAL APPRECIATION

I would like to thank a number of people who worked on this book as a joint project and contributed their talents, knowledge and time to make this the best book possible on the subject of Great Lakes Indian Clothing. To:

Loren Herrington - Thanks for sharing your knowledge, giving advice, and utilizing your time to help on this project.

Greg Hudson - Thanks for the wonderful illustrations that brought this book to life.

Joe Lee - Appreciation for your work on illustrations.

Mae Ring - Thanks for sharing your finger-weaving talent.

Dick Carney - In appreciation for your long-distance addition to the section on the history of finger-weaving.

Chuck Leonard - One of the finest silversmiths around, for your contribution of the section on the history of trade silver.

Dr. Nancy O'Lurie of the Milwaukee Public Museum - Thanks for your advice and suggestions.

Martin West, Director of Fort Ligonier, PA - Thanks for the time you spent showing the artifacts from the Fort and for the slide presentation on Eastern Indian Clothing.

Thanks to all who contributed to this project!

EDITOR'S PREFACE TO THE FIRST EDITION

This is the kind of book that an editor thoroughly enjoys! The author not only really knows her subject matter, but she is also anxious to impart her knowledge to her readers. That makes for a cooperative and fruitful relationship. And to make it more rewarding, the book is greatly needed and fills a gap in both the literature of the culture of the American Indian, and the arts and crafts of Native Americans.

In the middle 1980s, Ms. Hartman released, under a private limited printing, a small book about Great Lakes Indian clothing. As a serious student of the subject, she knew that there was a great need for information in the area, and that project met with great success. Still, Sheryl wanted to expand her efforts to cover subjects in a more thorough manner and to place the work with a publisher that would insure an availability of the work to the public at large. This well researched and written book is the product of that desire. This book should be of interest to anyone who desires accurate information about the Indians of North America.

In the process of preparing this volume for publication, illustrations were used by not only Greg Hudson and Joe Lee as noted on the cover, but also from the author and from R. L. Smith of Eagle's View Publishing. The text was proof read by Saundra Hansen and Brenda Martin who also made suggestions that, in no small way, added to this publication. We appreciate these contributions.

The author invites those who wish to obtain more information on the Great Lakes Indians or to arrange for an educational program about clothing, culture and daily life of the historic Indians of Indiana, Ohio, Michigan, Wisconsin or Illinois, to contact: Sheryl Hartman, Director - Indians of Indiana, P.O. Box 9563, Fort Wayne, IN 46899, hartman@parlorcity.com, 888/343-5344. To order woodland Indian clothing or illustrative work, contact Greg Hudson, 708 Garvey, Elsmere, KY 41018. To order finger-woven sashes, or if you want more information on woodland Indian primitive arts, contact Mae Ring, 3392 - 68th Street, Caledonia, MI 49316. Ralph Heath does quillwork, leatherwork, artwork and some clothing; while he does all period styles, he specializes in woodlands. He can be reached at 113 Cherry Street, Henryville, IN 47126, 812/294-4784.

We at Eagle's View Publishing hope you enjoy this instructive book and in many ways it is a testament to the tenacity of the culture of the American Indian. Many of the tribes whose homeland was situated in the Great Lakes Region continue to produce beautiful examples of ribbonwork and fingerweaving arts. The People, in some cases, have adopted contemporary craft supplies in their work, but the product remains truly and uniquely Native American. We continue to celebrate the culture of the American Indian - a culture that is viable in contemporary society. *MS*

INTRODUCTION

Students of Indian clothing can be deeply grateful to writers such as Samuel de Champlain, Nicholas Perrot, and Thomas McKeney and to artists such as Peter Rindisbacher, Charles Bird King, and George Winter, but they do long for more detailed descriptions. The clothing and adornment of the Great Lakes Indians, unlike the aboriginal style of the Plains, presents endless conjecture. Artifacts are pitifully few and scattered, and surviving examples are almost all without clear cut documentation. European contact came so early and influenced Indian dress so profoundly that few records remain.

The area covered in this work includes the regions surrounding the Great Lakes and the Ohio Valley. Tribes living in these areas include the Seneca, Delaware, Shawnee, Miami, Kickapoo, Piankeshaw, Illini, Peoria, Mascouten, Ottawa, Ojibwa, Algonquin, Huron, Menominee, and Eastern Dakota among others (See **Map** - *Figure 1*).

The Great Lakes Indians saw their clothing as more than an object of practical utility. They viewed it as an important form of self-expression. Imaginative clothing design could improve or modify their physical appearance and in the case of certain ceremonial dress, turn them into supernatural beings. The natural environment offered a variety of materials for construction and decoration and numerous possibilities for color and texture were available, as well as decorative materials capable of producing interesting sounds as the wearers moved about.

However, Native American clothing often served needs beyond those of basic protection and adornment. A garment could reveal its owner's political rank or social status by its design and ornamentation. In some tribal groups, certain clothing decorations were used to indicate the wearer's honored position within his family, his military prowess, his good deeds, or his membership in some special group. Also, in a part of the continent where religion tended to be a matter of individual expression, certain garments and accessories held complex sacred meaning.

Perhaps it was because the Indian people did take their clothing seriously and because they used it as a symbolic means of communication that they created such striking and varied costumes. In many instances, dress and personal decoration were successfully realized attempts to inspire awe, frighten an enemy, or command attention and admiration.

One fact emerges: identifying clothing by specific tribe was almost impossible among these related tribes. The *azian* or breechclout, for example, appears to have been worn by Indians almost everywhere. Contact among the tribes offered an opportunity for imitation in dress, and the trading of articles of clothing further confuses the issue.

By 1780, a sort of "*Pan-Indian*" material culture existed among the inhabitants of the Great Lakes Region. Trade goods such as wool blankets, silver brooches, iron and copper kettles, flintlock rifles, and metal tools were gifted and traded to the Indians. In exchange, the Indians provided furs, acted as guides, canoemen, built canoes, hunted, grew crops, and eventually signed their lands away to the whites. Housing for these people were wigwams and longhouses covered with bark, cattail mats and canvas from European ships.

According to ethnographers, other white chroniclers, and descendants of area Indians themselves, up through this era most materials used as clothing in the Great Lakes were tanned hides, leaves of plants, and a cloth woven of nettle fiber. The latter was woven in tubular form like the yarn bags used for underskirts by the women. The leaves were used as protection for one's head in hot weather and the tanned hides were used for making garments.

Some materials used instead of thread before the advent of the traders were nettle fiber twine, hemp twine, basswood twine and sinew. The nettle fibers could be twisted into fine or coarse thread as the occasion required. Instead of needles, the women used various pointed instruments (awls) made of thorns of the thornapple tree and the "splint bone" of a deer, to punch holes and feed the sinew through by hand.

RE-CREATING 18th AND 19th CENTURY WOODLAND INDIAN CLOTHING

Basically, trade cloth had replaced animal skins by the early 18th century. Linen, wool and cotton calico

FIGURE 1
DARKENED AREAS INDICATE GREAT LAKES WOODLAND INDIANS
Miami, Potawatomi, Ottawa, Chippewa, Kickapoo, Illini, Peoria, Shawnee,
Delaware, Menominee, Sauk, Fox, Mascouten, Algonquin, Winnebago,
Huron, Eastern Iowa and Eastern Sioux

Map: *U.S. Department of the Interior Arts and Crafts Board*

predominated historical Indian clothing in the Great Lakes. Galix, a linen fabric, and printed cotton calico were both popular items. Gimp was made of worsted silk or cotton twist with a cord or wire running through and was used for trimming and hair binding. These fabrics, basically cheap and drab, were dyed bright hues of red, blue and aurora in order to make them attractive to the natives.

In 1718, a French artist named Simon DuPratz painted a portrait of two Indian women wearing only wrap-around skirts made of deer or elk skin. This is one of the few remaining visual examples of wrap-arounds made of native materials. We can only guess how these skirts were actually embellished and decorated. Materials such as native earth and plant fiber paints, porcupine quills, and moose-hair embroidery were the most likely materials used in decoration. Woven skirts could have been made from plant fibers dyed with natural dyes and then decorated with quills or animal hair.

The earliest wool trade cloth received in North America came from France and England. The earliest trade was in better quality beaver cloths, such as kersey (lightweight) beaver cloth made in Kersey, England, gloucester cloth (Gloucester, England), and duffel (a heavy weight kersey from Duffel, Belgium). By 1800, most of the woolens traded in America were primarily made in Stroudwater, Gloucestershire, England, exclusively for American Indian consumption. This coarse "*strouding*," as it was called, usually was dyed scarlet red or dark navy blue (close to black). The woven cloth was dyed, rather than the yarn. Old blankets and other articles made from strouding have undyed selvages.

Original strouding can be identified by examining the peak of each triangular-shaped indentation of the selvage of white-edged cloth. In the original stroud cloth a hole will be found which was left from the heavy thread used to sew a cloth (usually canvas) binding along the edge, which in turn was clamped to the dyeing machine to permit the strouding, a "trade cloth," to act as a blotter and soak up the excess dye from higher quality material being dyed. Its being merely a blotter cloth explains its coarseness, the irregularity of the undyed selvage (the dye often running into the selvage), and the frequent spots that were not dyed all the way through - the middle of a cross section being left white.

Another old-style stroud cloth was the kind in which pieces of red and blue strouding have been attached along the white selvage edges. It might be repeated that early dyeing was far from colorfast, and early strouding often served as a source of dye for coloring porcupine quills, etc.

Stroud and duffles reportedly became available for native use immediately when trading began in the eastern Great Lakes region. According to the Sir William Johnson Papers, II, strouds were the first item mentioned in almost every list of gifts to the Indians. A better grade of woolen cloth was ratteen which was often used for coats; but, because of its thick twill and curled nap, it also made fine blankets. The ratteen appears in Johnson's list as ordered in deep purple.

Gifts presented to the natives also included *halfthick* which was found to be coarse material made in Lancashire. This material was probably used as cheap blankets since they were ordered in pieces, as were duffels and strouds.

ADORNMENT

DYES

Although European materials were being introduced and gradually replacing native made ones, the Indians to some extent maintained their skills in the use of dyes. Roots, buds, flowers, berries and seeds as well as juice from twigs, branches or bark gave up their special colors. Materials to be dyed were first boiled with the dye plant, rinsed, and if a darker hue was needed, boiled again. For setting the colors, a mordant such as mud or rusty water was added.

For reds there was the inner bark of the alder with bloodroot, or wild plum, and red ochre. Fresh bloodroot made yellow and orange, burr oak with hazel burrs, butternut bark and earth made black. For greens they used lamb's quarters; rotted maple gave purple, dried puccoon root made red face paint.

QUILLS

Porcupine quills, the major decorative material before the introduction of trade beads in the middle of the 17th century, were used in various ways. They were plaited (braided), woven, or wrapped to form stiff fringes or sewn into patterns. Some were used round, some flattened between the teeth or between thumb and forefinger. Moistened quills were then caught under and folded over the sinew thread. Stitches were never taken in the quills themselves for fear of splitting them with the "awl." Antler or smooth stone was often used to flatten the quills after the design was finished. Hunting pouches, knife sheaths, otterskin medicine bags and moccasins, among other items, were decorated with porcupine quills and used extensively in the 18th century. (About the best book available at this time on the use of porcupine quills in craft is *The Techniques of*

Porcupine Quill Decoration Among the Indians of North America by William C. Orchard.)

MOOSE-HAIR EMBROIDERY

Moose-hair embroidery, though not as widespread as quillwork, gained in popularity during the contact period. Most of the remaining examples of moose-hair embroidered objects are of Huron and Iroquois manufacture (*Flint Institute of Arts 1973*: pp. XXXVI-XXXVII).

The hair used in much of the embroidery comes from the mane, cheeks, and rump of the moose, and has an average length of about four to five inches. After the hair was collected, the hair was washed, dyed, moistened and flattened in much the same manner as porcupine quills. Techniques for working moose hair include line-work, zigzag line-work and twined weave.

TRADE BEADS

It was a natural progression to go from dyed quills and moose-hair embroidery to the trade beads for decoration. Soon they appeared on dresses, bags, pouches, moccasins, leggings, and garters in both the older geometric and later curvilinear patterns. Designs became less stylized and more recognizable as floral, geometric and double curve motifs.

Glass trade beads also quickly replaced traditional necklaces made from seeds, shells, bone and wood. Many sizes, shapes and colors attracted the Indians and they began wearing many strands of these at a time so that the front of a shirt or a woman's dress was ornamented by graduated rows of different colored beads, the whole decoration being five or six inches in depth. Some of the most popular trade beads presented to the Indians in the 18th century include white heart or Cornaline d'Aleppo, Chevron, Eye Beads, Russian faced blue beads, green melon beads, wound mulberry type, and red monochrome with a mixing of black in the glass among many others.

Beads were important in the early fur trade because they were compact and easily transportable. A six-foot string of small blue beads could purchase a beaver skin at Sault Ste. Marie in 1760. The first beads traded were large necklace size beads, then smaller "Pony" beads, suitable for sewing, and very small beads known as "seed beads" became popular.

Indian girls learned a number of stitching methods, including the "*overlaid*" or "*spot*" stitch and the "*lazy*" stitch. The overlaid or spot stitch was the most popular in the Great Lakes. Besides sewn beadwork, young girls learned to do woven work with or without a loom. Originally, they prepared plant fibers or sinew for this, but European cotton and linen threads soon replaced

FIGURE 2
QUILLED BAG
Elkskin
Wool Braid Trim - Red
Ring Brooches

4

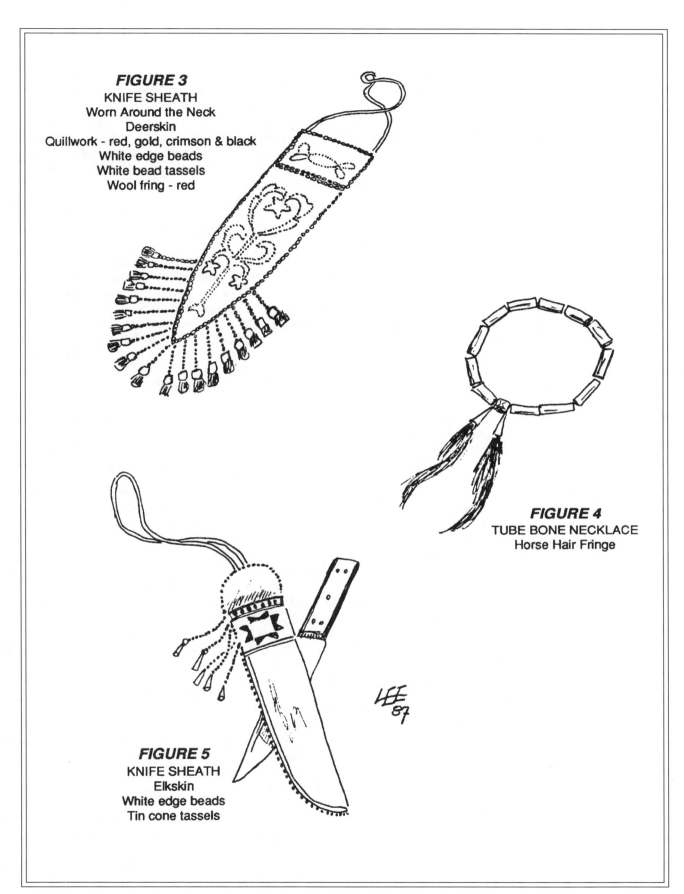

FIGURE 3
KNIFE SHEATH
Worn Around the Neck
Deerskin
Quillwork - red, gold, crimson & black
White edge beads
White bead tassels
Wool fring - red

FIGURE 4
TUBE BONE NECKLACE
Horse Hair Fringe

FIGURE 5
KNIFE SHEATH
Elkskin
White edge beads
Tin cone tassels

LEE
87

5

these. There were several types of looms used which include the bow loom, square or rectangular loom and the heddle loom that separated and alternated double warp threads in the weaving process (*Grand Rapids Public Museum* 1977: pp. 13-14).

An off-the-loom technique involved the use of white beads on a linen thread interwoven into finger-woven sashes, garters, and bags, which created zigzag, hexagonal or diamond patterns throughout the woven piece. Some examples of this 18th century technique can be found in the collections of the National Museum of Man in Ottawa, Canada.

As early as 1641, Father Isaac Joques dispensed gifts, including trade beads, in attempts to impart the Christian Faith to Indians who followed the Great Spirit and other deities. New converts to the Christian faith were likewise rewarded with beads for learning their lessons (*Kellogg*, pp. 23-25).

Another early form of beadwork was known as scroll bead applique which was curvilinear and geometric designs, usually in beads, sewn to the front of clothing. This was also an art form practiced to a great extent by eastern Algonquin Indians as well as by the Delaware, Micmac and Penobscot, among others. Although most of these tribes are associated with the Atlantic coastal regions, Delaware or Lene Lenape were pushed into the Lower Great Lakes Region during the 18th century.

Many of the designs created with beads were taken from old quillwork and moose-hair embroidery. Between 1750 and 1850 elaborate border designs were developed with the use of white beads on a dark trade cloth background. Extra color was introduced by running silk ribbons along the edge of the garment between the border and the white beadwork. Light blue and rose color ribbons were most commonly used. A floral design was introduced at the corners of the garment, thus adding a striking touch to wearing apparel (*Dehanadisonkwe* 1973: pp. 5-15).

A visual example of scroll bead applique may be seen in a painting by Benjamin West of William Penn's Treaty with the Delaware. The woman seated on the right is wearing a skirt and a matchcoat decorated with white beads in various designs. The scene is a treaty signed in 1683 in a village referred to as Shackamaxon, now a city park in Philadelphia. (An excellent book on how-to-do beadwork is *The Techniques of North American Indian Beadwork* by Monte Smith.)

TRADE SILVER

With the coming of silver trade articles, decoration took on new forms. Brooches were common. Of decorative-religious connotation were the double-barred crosses. These came in many sizes and were worn both as necklaces and ear bobs.

Much sought after were the circular discs, some of which measured twelve inches or more across. There were gorgets as well, breast ornaments patterned after those worn by army officers to represent, in the case of the army, the last vestige of armor. To the Indian, they were reminiscent of the old shell or slate gorgets, but these had sparkle and shine and were engraved with royal ciphers, animals, sunbursts and other designs. To some extent, these gorgets were small representations of the sacred alter of their religious and medicine societies. Silver bracelets, open at the back and pierced for tying on arms and legs, were used by both men and women.

Also of great importance were the peace medals which, unlike trade items, were presented to the chiefs and headmen in hopes of gaining their allegiance. The Indians often wore these medals during ceremonies and treaty negotiations (*Horan* 1972: pp. 185, 281, 293).

For a more indepth treatment of trade silver, see the article and illustrations by Chuck Leonard in this book.

BODY PAINTING

Body painting was the simplest kind of personal expression. It served many functions, one was that of protection against unfavorable climate. People living in areas of extreme temperatures often painted the face and exposed body parts with transparent oil or animal grease and some added red ground pigment to the grease as a protection against windburn. Most face and body paintings were, however, meant to accomplish something more than physical protection. Some were purely decorative, and others functioned in relation to some aspect of the wearer's culture whether it be his religion, personal accomplishments, or the social order and his place in it. In reality, some "*war paint*" usually was not a declaration of belligerency but a magic protective device. Other war paint was a declaration of hostile intentions and also served as a means of identifying friends from enemies. The art of face and body painting has been practiced for a good many other motives. In some tribes, symbolic face paintings were used to designate such temporary states as mourning, marriage or new paternity.

Before any face paint could be applied, the Indians had to pluck out their facial and body hair. They made tweezers from brass wire, which they always carried with them in their tobacco pouch. They plucked out their beards and the hair above their foreheads. This they did in a very quick manner, much like the plucking of a fowl, according to observations by John Heckewelder in 1762 (*Wallace* 1985: p. 54)

The men usually painted their faces in one of two methods: (**1**) the pattern was applied with paint to the

6

palm of the hand and transferred to the face by pressing the palm against it; or (**2**) the paint was applied solidly to the palm and a portion of the paint removed in a pattern, the palm then being pressed against the face. The paint generally used was colored earth, powdered and mixed with grease or oil. The face painting associated with several degrees of the Grand Medicine Lodge among the Chippewa is described as being one or two red stripes across the face for the First and Second degree Mide' and the Third degree having the upper half of the face green and lower half red. The Fourth degree was noted by painting the left half of the face green with red spots and wearing eagle feathers painted red (*Densmore* 1979: p. 93).

TATTOOING

Tattooing was still in use in the mid-18th century and John Long, a captive of the Mohawks, described its execution during a Chippewa adoption ceremony. "The candidate first sweats ... then is led to the Chief's house wherein he is extended on his back. The chief draws the figure he intends to make with a pointed stick dipped in water in which gunpowder has been dissolved; after which, with ten needles dipped in vermillion and fixed in a small wooden frame, he pricks the delineated parts, and where the bolder outlines occur he incises the flesh with gunflint. The vacant spaces, or those not marked with vermillion, are rubbed in with gunpowder, which produces a variety of red and blue; the wounds are then smeared with punkwood to prevent them from festering." (*Bender* 1980: p. 16)

Tattooing was also observed by Heckewelder among the Delaware. "They have poplar bark in readiness burnt and reduced to a powder, the figures that are to be tattooed are marked or designed on the skin; the operator with a small stick ... to the end of which some sharp needles are fastened, quickly pricks over the whole so that blood is drawn, then a coat of this powder is laid and left on to dry. Before the whites came into this country, they scarified themselves for this purpose with sharp flint stones or pricked themselves with the sharp teeth of a fish." (*Wallace* 1985: pp. 54-55)

FINGER-WEAVING

Drawings done by white artists at the beginning of the 18th century show the use of braiding, netting, looping, weaving or twilling of pack straps, garter, belts, sashes, and storage bags and pouches. The garters and sashes were woven in varying patterns and sizes. Sashes, although usually worn as belts or bandolier straps, were also used as head wrappings for both men and boys in a turban fashion. (*Viola* 1976: pp. 40, 95, 97)

The history and techniques of finger-weaving are treated in some detail in the articles by Dick Carney and Mae Ring located in the *Appendix* of this book.

WOODLAND DESIGNS
HOW NATIVE PEOPLE VIEWED THEIR WORLD

Designs for clothing, bags, knife sheaths, medicine bags, baskets, bark containers, twined bags, quivers, moccasins, burden straps, slave ties, etc. were utilized in most cases for more than mere decoration. In fact, most embellishment effectively symbolized membership in certain societies; accomplishment in deed; acquired position; status; age; ability or skill level; ritual spirit or entity; and on and on in such a way that many were kept secret to all in the village but the owner. Some symbols were considered sacred and cherished for good use, others were used for something negative and some were used to inflict injury, bad will or pain.

Designs often symbolized simple basic concepts in Great Lakes Societies such as generosity, sharing and respect for the individual, self-respect and independence. These values extended beyond human relationships to the surrounding world of nature. Native people expressed their belief in the need to live on terms of mutual respect with the animals upon which they depended to survive, and with the spiritual forces, which controlled the animals, the stars and the seasons of the year. Those spiritual forces were referred to as Manitos.

The activities of the manitos and their places of power in the universe were structured by myth. These mythological stories recounted the creation of the world and activities of the great cultural hero Nanabozho. Myths revealed to the individual the basic structure of the cosmos and gave him knowledge of how to interpret and control the forces among which he moved.

According to the belief of the Natives of the Great Lakes the universe consisted of three parallel worlds. The earth was at the center, which was considered to be a large island floating on a great lake. Below the waters of the lake was the underworld dominated by extremely powerful manitos that controlled the plants, animals and fish of land and water. The most powerful of these underworld manitos were the Underwater Panthers which were composite beings, each with a horned head, the body of a cat and long, scaled dragon-like tails. These beings could bestow good things such as the healing medicines that grew in the earth but they were also closely associated with danger and destruction. Sorcerers gained the power for evil from the underworld spirits and dangerous storms arose on the lakes when the Underwater Panther swirled his tail, overturning canoes and drowning travelers.

7

Above the earth arched the huge dome of the sky, beyond which lay the upper world which was dominated by equally powerful spirits called Thunderbirds. These manitos could bestow success in war and other such goodwill,. The thunder and lightning were supposed to be created by the flashing of their eyes and flapping of their wings, bringing the rain that made plants grow.

At the time of creation, Nanabozo battled with both powers from above and below and through his victories over them came the ability to hunt and control the animals by men.

The Great Lakes Indians also honored another set of equally powerful spirits or manitos, the spirits of the Four Winds, which blew from the north, south, east and west. The four winds controlled the seasons, bringing changes in weather that sustained the life cycle. The center of the axis of the four sacred directions was the path or opening from earth into the worlds above and below.

Thus we come back to the art and designs which diagram these cosmic structures and fix the locations of spirit powers in the universe. The meaning of the designs or visual imagery depended on the interpretation of the motifs used and the way they were placed in relation to each other. In other words, taking certain symbols, designs or concepts out of context, they lose some or all of their meaning within the spiritual cosmos that they originated. In order to establish paths of communication with the spirit world it was necessary to create artifacts that correctly and harmoniously replicated the universal order.

1 - MEDICINE BAGS OR BUNDLES

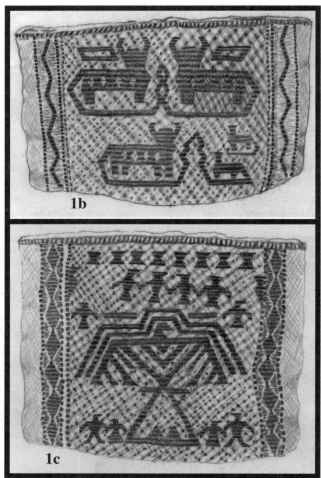
1b

1c

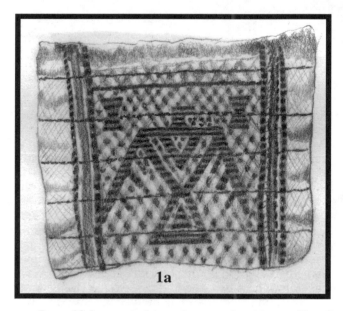
1a

Beautiful woven bags decorated with motifs of THUNDERBIRDS on one side and UNDERWATER PANTHERS on the underside with the contents stored inside which have been granted to humans to use in the middle realm of earth reflect the three zones of the universe. These motifs symbolized the power contained within the bag which could be activated to destroy enemies, heal the sick, aid in locating animals and to cast spells of love or hate. The potent objects contained in medicine bundles transferred some of this power to the people.

2. THUNDERBIRD POWER LINES

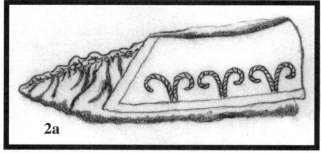
2a

The spirit beings are often surrounded by "power lines" that show how their forces are manifested in the universe. Thunderbirds are shown usually with jagged zigzag lines, which represent the thunder, and lightning they generate. OPPOSING DOUBLE HOOKS: Seen on bags and moccasin flaps appear to represent the thunderbird

2b

especially since the opposing hooks on one pair of moccasin flaps form explicit images of thunderbirds.

3. UNDERWATER PANTHER POWER LINES

3

The underworld deities whip up the waters with the lashing of their long tails and are usually depicted adjacent to wavy or castellated lines that express their movement. The whirlpool was a sign of the presence of this spirit and patterns of CONCENTRIC CIRCLES, POLYGONS and SQUARES can be seen as images of underworld power.

4. MEDICINE BAGS WITH ABSTRACT GEOMETRIC DESIGNS

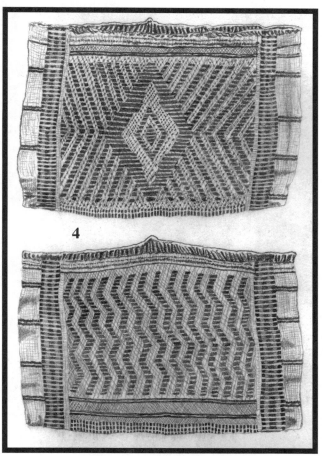

4

Some medicine bags combine representations of Thunderbirds or Underwater Panthers on one side with ABSTRACT GEOMETRIC DESIGNS on the reverse side. These probably were intended to express the energy and power that emanated from the supernatural beings. SUN: The sun is seen in many Great Lakes tribes as a motif, It appears as the central image painted on Naskapi and Eastern Cree ceremonial hides. In some Eastern Sub-Arctic compositions the sun is seen by a quillwork circle or a series of concentric circles with projecting rays suggesting a connection between the plants and animal growth and the power of the sun. There are similar motifs on a Shawnee bag dating from the 19th century as well as pipestems, wampum gorgets, silver gorgets, drums, moccasins and pouches.

5. POUCHES

A number of pouches exhibit abstract symbolic

5

representation. Some contain panels of netted quillwork at the bottom containing hourglass forms, which are probably simplified Thunderbird representations. There are others that have quillwork-embroidered motifs suggestive of horned serpents, companions of the underwater panthers. Linked chevrons are also reminiscent of the serpentine motifs. When the belt pouches were worn, overall asymmetrical designs seem to set up an opposition between the two spirit worlds. Belt pouches folded over the belt so that two halves of the design field formed front and back surfaces when the pouch was worn.

6. EQUAL ARMED CROSS

6

This was another motif frequently used by Great Lakes artists. This symbolized the Four Sacred Directions of Mother Earth. It was associated with locating the central axis of the cosmos so humans could communicate with the spirit world. Sometimes the crosses are juxtaposed with circles - a motif that is said possibly represents the openings into the upper and underworlds. Example: A bear effigy pipe collected before 1809 in the Great Lakes has an inlaid lead cross surrounding the circular stem opening. It is oriented to face the smoker as he sent his offering of tobacco to the realm of the spirits through the circle in the center of the cross.

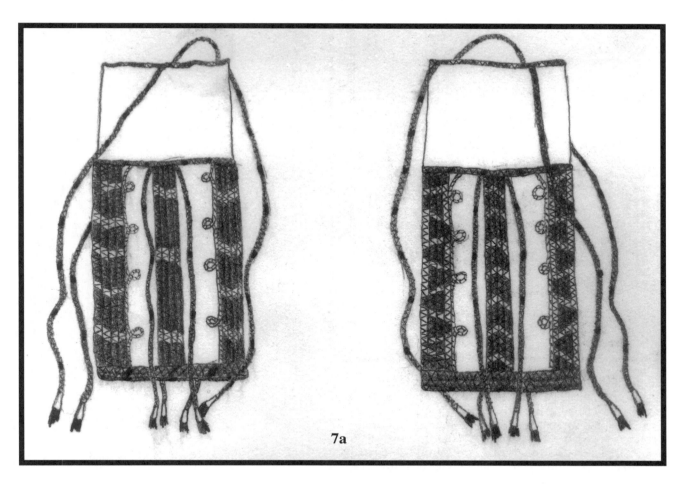

7a

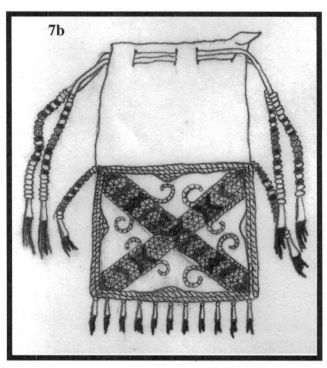

7b

7. EXTREME STYLIZATION AND USE OF ABSTRACT SYMBOLS

Sometimes it is difficult to determine whether geometric patterns refer to underworld or upper world figures or manitos. Bands of zigzag lines merge into wave patterns, the bodies of the Thunderbirds become hourglass forms and their linked wings fade into a single contour line. The upper half of an Underwater Panther dissolves into rows of castellated lines that might also suggest the bottom halves of Thunderbird torsos. Much of this uncertainty about these motifs seems intentional on the part of the artists. TRANSFORMATION OF OUTER APPEARANCE OF MANITOS: Myths repeatedly make references to the ability of manitos to change their appearance assuming human or animal form, or they could appear as rays of light, disembodied sound, or even feelings. The ambiguous forms now take new forms that neither represent the recognized form or the symbolic form instead actually dissolving into a complete abstract based upon the transformation of such forms in dreams or a new reality envisioned by the artist.

8. DREAMS

Patterns and ornaments were often revealed in dreams or visions and painted, carved, woven or applied to an

11

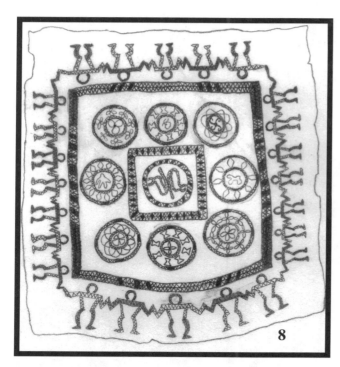

8

individual's clothing or weapons to display the power of guardian spirits. These were often abstract versions of those described in this article or personal spirits that were depicted in abstract form and the meaning only known to the owner. Example: A Miami woman who had lost friends and relatives when Iroquois attacked her village had a dream that her people would lead a large war party and defeat the enemy. She apparently saw in her dream that she was to wear a "kind of apron of deer skin dressed black, before and behind, and her flesh was also painted black." The black dye or paint was composed of walnut hulls and iron filings and was often used to dye clothing, knife sheaths and pouches; this she used probably as camouflage since the attack occurred at night when her people "fell suddenly upon the sleeping Iroquois... "

9. MIDEWIWIN DESIGNS

An intertribal religious society formed in the Great Lakes which made use of special artistically

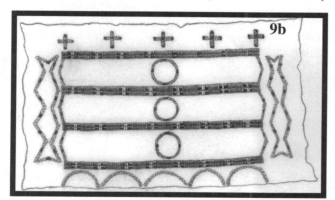

9b

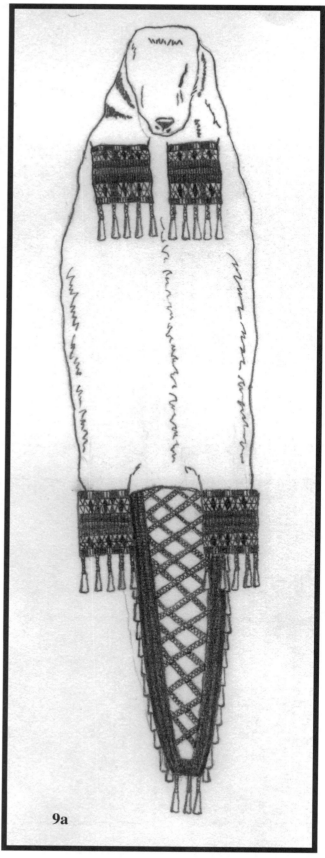

9a

embellished objects during ritual performances and ceremonies which were carefully protected in secrecy from all but a privileged few whites. Robes were known to have been used by members probably as instructive charts demonstrating the distribution of spirit powers in the cosmos, and as a testimony to mystical out-of-body journeys through the universe that they experienced. Some may also have been worn as cloaks in the manner described by military officers, with the designs on the inside to preserve their semi-secret powers. One robe that appears in *Patterns of Power* exhibits four horizontal bands outlined by quilled borders that may represent the subdivision of the upper and underworlds into four zones of power. The circles may represent the openings between earth and the upper and underworlds, the "holes in the sky" through which the shaman's soul entered the spirit world during trances. Crosses establish the central universal axis and the four sacred directions of mother earth and the wavy lines and serpentine forms on the edges of the composition perhaps refer to underwater powers which the shaman controlled.

10. HEADDRESS

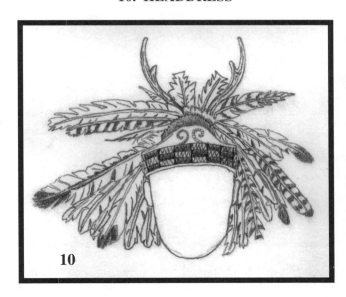

10

Made from the head and antlers of a deer and was possibly used in a shamanistic context similar to one described as used by a Miami shaman in front of a British officer at Fort George or Amhertsburg. The description of this headdress leads to the conclusion that the designs used in bags, pouches and robes can also be applied to the construction detail of a headdress. The headdress has a prominent red disk above the upper world motif of opposed double hooks which would represent the powerful sun manitos. It and the many eagle feathers fringing the headdress, have been trimmed to form a spiked zigzag contour. It is possible to conclude that these lines are power lines similar to those on woven bags and pouches.

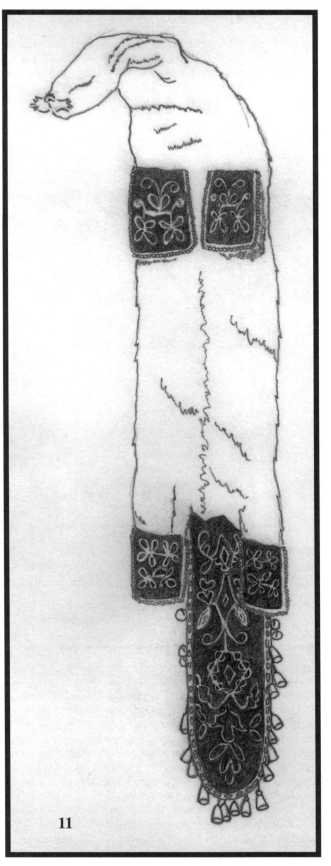

11

11. FLORAL PATTERNS

Floral imagery did not come to dominate Great Lakes art until the late 19th century and most likely has its origins in traditional beliefs about the supernatural power existing in certain plants. It is very probable that floral patterns no matter how highly stylized contained references to manitos power controlled by the owners of the objects, just as did images of power animals (Illustration on previous page).

12. ART OF DRESS

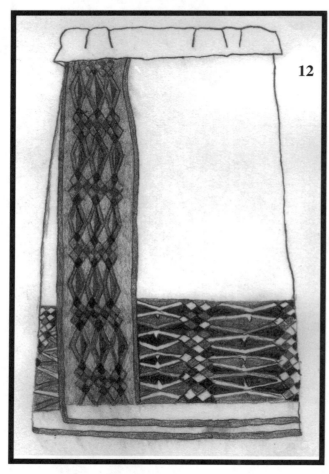

The use of contrasting patterns such as underworld figures and upper world figures is often seen. Silk ribbon appliqué provided a new material to utilize traditional motifs such as the juxtaposition of two bands of different geometric patterns of ribbon borders sewn onto moccasin flaps, leggings and skirts. On many moccasins the two cuffs display contrasting patterns and color combinations. The same type of overall design is seen on the front and back wing flaps of leggings and on the bottom and side borders of skirts and breechclouts. Again this contrast of colors and motifs was used to express the belief in the balanced opposition of the two major powers in the universe.

13. ORNAMENTED DRESS

Great Lakes people who demonstrated great skills, abilities or bravery were given silver brooches, crosses and earwheels, wampum, vermilion, silk ribbonwork, quillwork bags which displayed their personal powers that helped them, and embellished their clothing with the same nervous, energized patterns of wavy and zigzag lines used to represent the powers of the supernatural world, alluding to the individual's links to the manitos.

14. DESIGNS EXPLAINED THROUGH DANCE AND ORATION

Many items such as wampum belts, certain bags, robes, war clubs, pipes and quilted ornaments could only be explained through the additional use of special dances, music rich dress and special stories that communicated

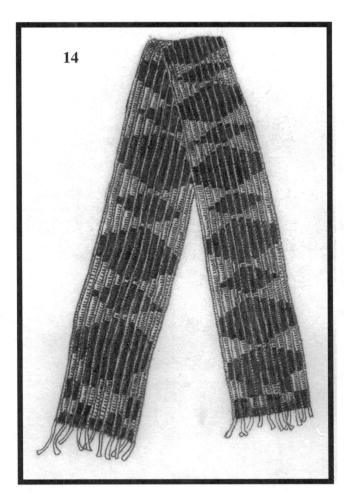

14

the ritual use of the item displayed.

15. DESIGN CONFUSION

Military officers that were stationed at forts throughout the Great Lakes were sometimes responsible for making journals collecting information as well as artifacts from Great Lakes people. Often the number of Indians visiting the fort was staggering, numbering in the thousands and representing nearly a dozen tribes, among the Chippewa, Potawatomi, Shawnee, Miami, Wyandot, Cherokees, Mississauga, Fox, Delaware, Ottawa and Mohawk which complicates matters when trying to document which artifacts were left behind by which groups of people. Further, many articles of clothing and ritual objects were probably acquired through fur traders and fellow officers who had contact with groups of Cree, Metis, and other Canadian peoples living north and west of the Great Lakes. This added more complications to identitifying tribal affiliation with certain designs or particular pieces of art. Finally, intermarriage or adoption of tribal members from different tribes undoubtedly resulted in a great deal of interborrowing among the artistic traditions of the Great Lakes region. Gift giving which was a major part of daily life, resulted in an exchange of artifacts among the Indian people as well.

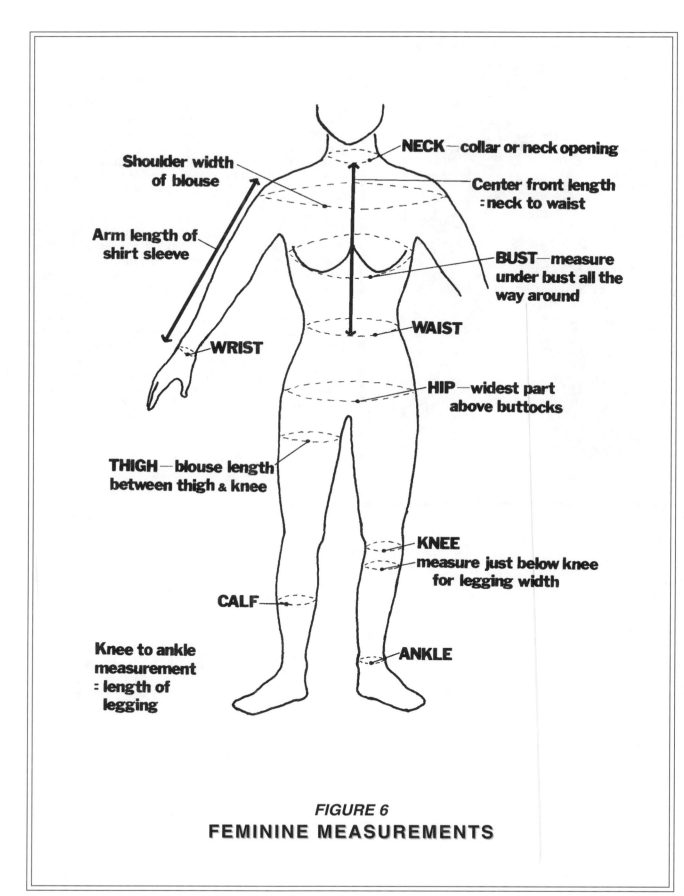

FIGURE 6
FEMININE MEASUREMENTS

WOMEN'S CLOTHING

INTRODUCTION

Clothing styles were similar for most Great Lakes Indian women. The real differences were in the treatment of the garment with ornamentation which was based in part on the individual ability and resources for the materials needed. The chiefs and sachems were responsible for the distribution of annuity payments and were usually the first ones to meet with the traders who furnished the goods. Those who did not stand in good favor with a leader or who were not influential with the white trader, did not always receive the choice merchandise. Often women and children were not included on payroll and payment lists, so they received what was left over (*Blackburn* 1942: pp. 392-393).

In giving presents during the 18th century, the donors adhered to the rule of precedence in rank. The common Indian's wife received only a piece of stroud to be used for a blanket and petticoat. The stroud, being a cheap cloth made of woolen rags, was quite different from the fine material given to the chief's wife. The chief and sachems were frequently the beneficiaries of special goods such as clothing and jewelry for their families (*New York Colonial Documents*, VII: p. 186).

In contrast, those Indian women who were involved in tribal politics and had a say in the activities of the warriors often made requests for specific items such as smaller size blankets, scarlet hose, lively colored calicoes, ribbons and gartering. Color listings for textiles and laces included such hues and shades as deep red, deep blue, green, scarlet and yellow. Silk handkerchiefs, silver rings, ear bobs and barley corn beads also found their way into feminine hands. These items portrayed the brighter side of life for the women (*Jacobs* 1967: pp. 46-47).

A letter dated January 8, 1783 to Francios Bosseron at Vincennes from Pierre Latoure at Petit-Duabache (trading post in central Indiana) included a complaint that the merchandise was too expensive. Even with enticement, the Indians refused to trade (*Lasselle Papers*, Charles B 1781-1785: p. 165). Knowledge of the suitability of trade items was considered to be essential to the success of trade with Indians. From the time of the treaty of Lancaster in 1748, presents of textiles and hardware and munitions were to be used for securing warriors in preparation for the eventual conflict between the French and the British for control of the New World. This gave the Indians the opportunity to demand the best from both sides.

WRAP-AROUND SKIRT AND BLANKET

Throughout the eastern United States, the basic garment of native women was a wrap-around skirt. It was worn from Georgia north into Quebec and as far west as eastern Kansas and Minnesota. Prehistoric stone and ceramic sculptures from the east indicate that the wrap-around skirt may in fact have been one of the most long lasting and widely worn of all Native American clothing forms. Until the 18th century, these garments were made from native woven cloth or animal skins. Possibly a few women living adjacent to Europeans had skirts of trade cloth (*Cumming* 1972: pp. 272-273, 285).

Records from the mid-18th century indicate the skirts worn by the Indian women were made from trade cloth. "...they have a short blue petticoat, which reaches to their knees and the brim of which is bordered with red or other ribbons..." (*Kalm* 1772: p. 116). John Heckewelder, who traveled among the Ohio Country Delaware and Mohicans, observed that the women, at the expense of their husbands or lovers, lined their petticoats with blue or scarlet cloth blankets or covering with choice ribands of various colors, or with gartering on which they fixed a number of silver brooches, or small round buckles. They adorned the leggings in much the same manner (*Pannabecker* 1986).

Reverend David Zeisberger refers to the clothing of the Indian women as follows: "...the dress which particularly distinguishes the women is a petticoat or stroud; blue, red or black, made of a piece of cloth about two yards long, adorned with red, blue or yellow bands laid double and bound about the body." In the same paragraph, Zeisberger refers to these bands as being of silk and also calls them ribbon. No design or technique is mentioned (*Pannebecker* 1986).

Heckewelder adds that "the wealthy adorn themselves besides with ribands and gartering of various

17

1683 DELAWARE WOMAN

SOURCE: Painting by Benjamin West of William Penn's Treaty with the Delaware Indians in 1683 at Philadelphia, PA

Headband - Rows of Quillwork sewn to Leather or Bark Backing

Matchcoat - Brain-tanned elk or deer skin dyed with walnut hulls and iron filings to create black or dark brown color

Shirt - No shirt is shown in the original painting

Skirt - Brain-tanned elk or deer skin dyed with walnut hulls/iron filings

Leggings - Black dyed deer or elkskin is used for the tight fitted tubular leggings, each featuring an outer wing edged with white quills

Moccasins - Center seam decorated with quillwork; white bead applique on flaps and around quillwork

Bead Applique - both geometric and double curve motif styles are shown. Double curve motif was used extensively by the Penobscot, Micmac and Iroquois; sometimes as a symbol of civil and social bonds holding the people of the tribe together (*Speck 1970: pp. 69-71*)

FIGURE 7

FIGURE 7

19

Blanket — Stroud

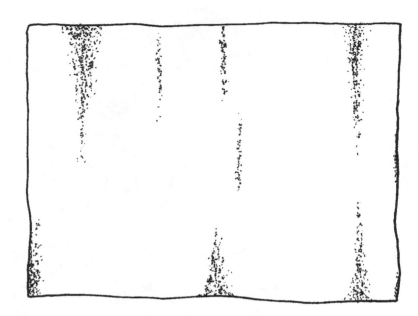

FIGURE 8
WRAP-AROUND
SKIRT

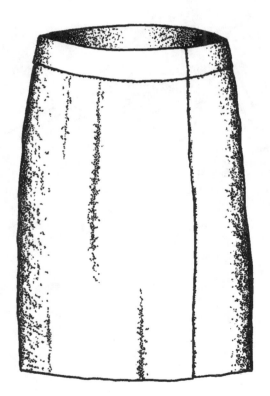

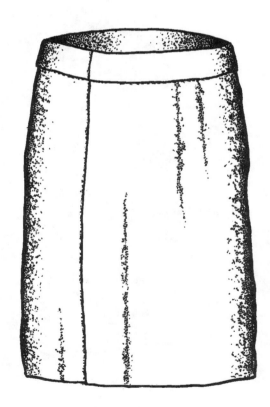

Overlaps right over left

Overlaps left over right

colors, beads and silver brooches. These ornaments are arranged by the women, who, as well as the men, know how to set themselves off in style ..."

"Delaware men pay particular attention to the dress of their women, and on that account clothe themselves rather meanly. There are many who think it scandalous to appear better clothed than their wives," John Heckewelder observed in 1762. Delaware men love to see their wives well clothed, which is a proof that they are fond of them, at least in Heckewelder's estimation (*Wallace* 1985: p. 56).

In 1788, a painting by Thomas Davies reveals that Huron women of Quebec wore brightly printed calico trade shirts over wrapped skirts. The skirts reveal ribbon edging and on some, alternate use of colors (*Schoolcraft* 1980: p. 145).

"Women wore petticoats, reaching below the knee. The fabric was stroud which was first washed giving the fabric a chance to shrink to produce a felt-like feel and look. Some also wore garments of printed linen or cotton of various colors, decorated at the breast with a great number of silver buckles, which are also worn by some as ornaments upon their petticoats... They adorn

their ears, necks and breasts with corals, small crosses, little round escutcheons, and crescents, made either of silver or wampum" according to Loskiel in 1794 (Loskiel, G. H., *History of the Missions of United Brethren Among the Indians of N. America*: by CI. LaTrobe).

A vivid description of early clothing worn by a bride at Michilimackinac was praised by editor R. G. Thwaites as Mrs. Baird reminiscences about the wedding garment worn in 1819: "The skirt reached about half-way between the ankle and the knee, and was elaborately embroidered with ribbon and beads on both the lower and upper edges. Above this horizontal trimming were rows upon rows of ribbon, four or five inches wide, placed so near together that only a narrow strip of cloth showed like a narrow cord. Accompanying this was worn a pair of leggins made of broadcloth ... the embroidery about three inches from the side edge. Around the bottom the trimming is between four and five inches in width. The moccasins, also, were embroidered with ribbons and beads." Baird noted that similar ensembles were worn by the bride's Indian mother, and two women traders of French and Ottawa extraction.

STRAP DRESS

Frances Densmore obtained descriptions from Minnesota Chippewa Indians of women's clothing from the early fur trade period. "In early times the clothing of a woman consisted of a binary garment made of two deerskins, one forming the front and the other forming the back of the dress, the two parts being fastened together at the shoulders and held in place by a belt" (*Densmore* 1979: p. 31).

What may have been the earliest form of a binary dress, the strap dress, once worn from Northeast Canada and west to the foothills of the northern Rockies, was noted by Alexander Mackenzie as early as the 1790s. Made from two large pieces of leather trimmed into rectangles, sewn together along the sides and supported by shoulder straps; this version of the binary dress covered the wearer from above the breast to mid-calf (*Conn* 1974).

Richard Conn of the Denver Art Museum made this comment about the extensive use of the strap dress throughout the northern Great Lakes and prairies: "... the strap dress was often worn with separate leather sleeves. The use of these removable sleeves in a climate which would rarely require their removal is difficult to explain except in terms of the limited availability of hides..." (*Conn* 1974).

When the traders brought broadcloth, a woman might have made a similar dress of cloth, but she always

had a dress of hides for use when she was at work. To this were added moccasins, leggings and a blanket. Four kinds of broadcloth were carried by these early traders and used to make the strap dresses and leggings. The cheapest quality was dark blue, coarse stroud cloth with a white border. Enough of this for a woman's dress cost the equivalent of five ($5.00) dollars in furs. The three other kinds cost about double that amount and were (**1**) Jet Black broadcloth which was very fine and shiny, (**2**) a brownish broadcloth with a border of narrow stripes, and (**3**) a bright scarlet broadcloth. To these fabrics should be added gray list cloth and white list cloth (*Densmore* 1979: pp. 30-33).

The amount purchased for a woman's dress was the length from her armpits to her ankles with about a half of a yard additional. The early trade cloth was not always wide enough to give the desired fullness, so the additional length was cut into pieces and put in the front of the dress as a front breadth. The traders brought worsted braids in various colors and silk ribbons and several rows of these were put across the front of the dress and called a "rainbow." Later a more abundant use of color braid arose and this was put around the lower edge of the dress (*Densmore* 1979: pp. 31-33).

Again, this garment was held in place by strips of cloth over the shoulders and confined at the waist by a belt or sash. Arms coverings were usually provided and

FIGURE 9

FIGURE 10

could be worn or laid aside as desired. These consisted of two pieces of cloth fastened at the wrist after the manner of a cuff, and the two pieces attached at the back of the neck, forming a cape-like protection to the shoulders. When calico was brought by the traders, a loose fitting calico sacque (gown or jacket) was frequently worn over the above described dress without the arm covering (*Densmore* 1979: pp. 30-33).

Peter Rindisbacher offered a unique view of Chippewa daily life as well as the dress of the occupants of the Minnesota villages of the 1820s. Strap dresses appear quite common among the females that were made of two colors of wool - gray dresses with red wool sleeves and trim, or blue dresses with red sleeves and blue trim (*American Heritage* 1970: pp. 34-47).

Even into the 1830s strap dresses continued in use among the Great Lakes tribes. For example, in one painting in the National Collection of Fine Arts, Smithsonian Institution, Washington, D.C., a Chippewa woman poses with a child in a cradleboard wearing a dark wool strap dress decorated with silk ribbons and brooches.

STRAP DRESS PATTERN

The style illustrated here is referred to as the Ojibway Strap Dress due to the fact that this dress appears most often among the Saulteaux Ojibway during the early 19th century. The trade cloth strap dress of the 18th century originated from a three-skin dress of the pre-contact period. It was worn from Canada south to the Ohio Valley and from the east coast to the northern plains.

The original skin dress was made by attaching two skins front to back and a third forming the sleeves and straps needed to complete the dress (*Figure 11*). The trade cloth dress was made from 3-4 yards of wool fabric.

When making a strap dress, use stroud cloth or wool with soft nap and keep in mind that this will rub directly on your skin unless it is lined with linen or cotton fabric. Measure hips and add 1 1/2" for seam allowance and freedom of movement.

1 - Select 3-4 yards of wool fabric 45" to 60" wide folded in half lengthwise. Cut two pieces for dress body and sew sides together so that the seam is on the wrong side. This forms a tube that fits just over the breasts to the middle of the calf of the leg.

2 - A shoulder strap should be attached to the front and back of the tube over each shoulder. These should fasten with a button in front so that dress removal is made easier. The straps extend 4" down the front beyond the button to form decorative tabs. The fabric for the straps can be of a different color than the body of the dress. (*American Heritage* 1973)

3 - Detachable sleeves fasten in back with a button below the neck and with a strap across the front. Sleeve length can be determined by measuring from wrist to shoulder center where the sleeve would rest comfortably. To determine the extended width of the sleeve, measure from underneath the arm around to the center of the back and add that measurement to the length of the sleeve to get a total length needed for detachable sleeves.

4 - Edges of sleeves, straps and hem may be trimmed with silk ribbons or military braid. Straps and skirt can be decorated with silver brooches. Cut ribbonwork applique could be added if portraying a post-1800 Indian woman. Tin cones or brass hawk bells could also be used on the hem with or without white edge beading. Adding a finger-woven sash around the waist gives shape to the dress and embellishment. Leggings could be added to complete the ensemble.

WOMEN'S LEGGINGS

The female woodland Indians wore leggings quite similar to those of the male. Generally, women's leggings were listed as being short, only coming up to the knee and held in place with garters. In the harsh winter months, women would also wear the long leggings over the knee to further protect the legs. The fabrics used were stroud, ratteen, duffle and penistone (*Jacobs* 1967: p. 49).

Leggings were made from half a width of stroud cloth blanket during the 18th century, which was the reason for the short style worn just over the knee. This changed after the Revolutionary War when trade picked up and a demand was made for better and larger blankets.

In 1762, a Delaware woman was buried in her finery including "...scarlet leggins decorated with different colored ribands sewed on, the outer edge being finished off with small beads also of various colors ..." This observation was made by John Heckewelder who stayed with the Mohawk and Delaware Indians (*Wallace* 1985: p. 59).

Illustrations of Chippewa women in the 1820s show leggings worn tight around the leg with a wing or flap on the outside trimmed in ribbons. The wing often curved slightly inward at the ankle. The leggings were positioned just inside the top of the moccasins (*American Heritage* 1970: pp. 30-49).

The following are some illustrations of some vari-

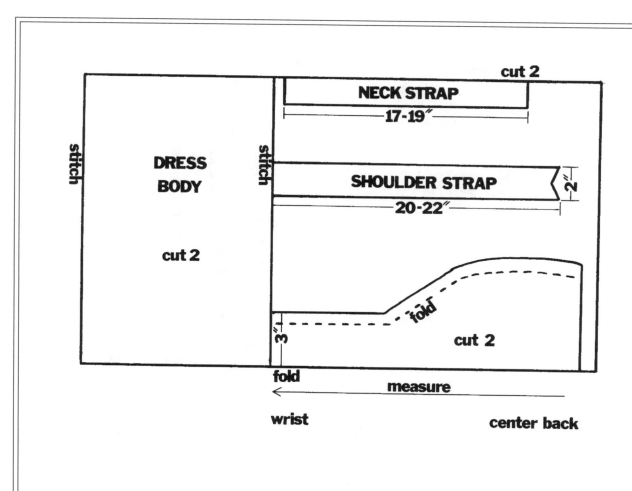

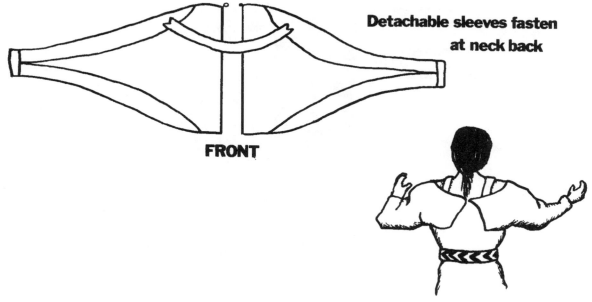

Detachable sleeves fasten at neck back

FRONT

FIGURE 11
STRAP DRESS

SIDE SEAM

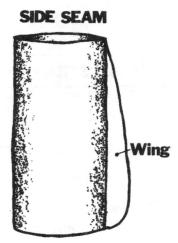

Wing

CENTER SEAM

↑Back of legging

Tight fit to
shape of leg.

Tie garter just
below knee.

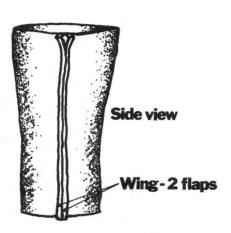

Side view

Wing - 2 flaps

FIGURE 12
WOMEN'S LEGGINGS
18th Century Styles

ations of the woman's leggings as used by these respective tribes:

FIGURE 13

MIAMI STYLE

Garter

POTAWATOMI STYLE

FIGURE 14

Miami Style - These leggings were made from matching or contrasting wool (i.e., same as the skirt or another color) or of broadcloth. They were tube-shaped fitting just below the knee and held in place with a garter. Although it depended upon the size of the leg of the wearer, the average size is 22" around and about 15" long. The selvage edge is placed at the top and will naturally be hidden by the skirt when worn. The leggings are sewn into a tube so that a snug fit is obtained. Ribbonwork is applied to the outside of the leggings and around the hem and bottom. As with skirts, beads are sometimes used as edging and silver buttons applied above the ribbonwork in a variety of patterns such as diamonds, stars, clusters, etc.

Delaware Style - In this style, the leggings are sewn into a tube so that a flap is made to which ribbonwork is applied. A flap about 3" wide is sufficient, and a 1"

ribbon binding may be applied to edges and then beads used as a decorative trim if desired. Again, they are kept in place with a garter.

FIGURE 15

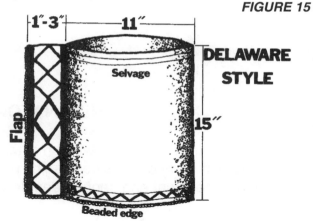

1"-3" 11"
Flap Selvage DELAWARE STYLE 15"
Beaded edge

Ojibwa Style - These are a tube fitted and narrowed at the ankle with tapered wing flap. They were often embellished similarly to those of the Miami and Potawatomi styles with ribbons and beads. This style was well illustrated by Peter Rindisbacher in a painting that was done in the 1820s.

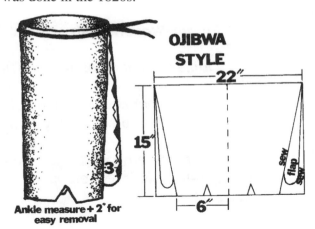

OJIBWA STYLE

22"
15" 3" SEW flap SEW
6"
Ankle measure + 2" for easy removal

FIGURE 16

These styles were also worn by the Kickapoo, Illini, Peoria, Shawnee, Huron, Ottawa, Mascouten and other tribes around the Great Lakes in the 18th and 19th centuries.

Of further note is that, according to Sir William Johnson in 1755, "Women's scarlet hose with clocks were in demand." Often, military issue cotton stockings were presented to the Indians and used in place of stroud leggings.

INDIAN WOMAN 1745-1760

View of an Indian woman of the French and Indian War period shows her utilizing the white man's trade shirt in a plain white or solid color with wrap-around skirt or petticoat and center seam leggings.

Hair - Tied in a single braid behind her head

Silver Ear Wheels - Five (5) hanging from each ear

Ruffled Linen Shirt - Worn over skirt held at neck with silver brooch; decorated on each shoulder with 1/2 inch ring brooches

Finger-Woven Sash - Tied at the waist over the shirt

Quilled Knife Sheath and Knife - This hangs from the sash

Wrap-Around Skirt - Made of wool stroud and decorated with silver ring brooches at hem and single strip of wool braid or silk folded over the hem edge

Center Seam Leggings - Constructed of matching or contrasting color and decorated with silver brooches on each side of the seam, then tucked into moccasin tops

Moccasins - Center seam moccasins with wing flaps decorated with quillwork, tin cones and red-dyed deer hair fringe

FIGURE 17

FIGURE 17

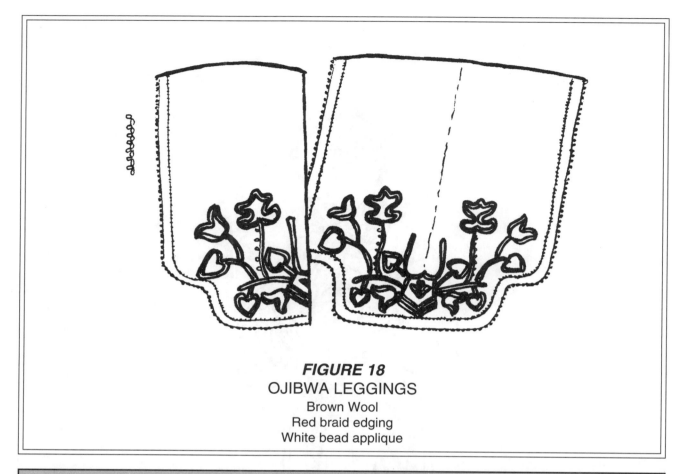

FIGURE 18
OJIBWA LEGGINGS
Brown Wool
Red braid edging
White bead applique

WOMEN'S SHIRT

In the 18th century, trade shirts of calico, linen and muslin were issued to Indian men and women living in the Great Lakes area. These shirts, whether printed or plain, were styled in the manner of European shirts of the period and a pattern for making this style shirt may be found in the section on men's clothing.

The shirts were usually very full, made from a square cut body design allowing the shoulder seams to drop over the upper arm. A gusset was placed on each side of the neck opening and under each arm for added comfort. Most had a collar that folded over the back of the neck. Some added cuff ruffles and a front ruffle around the center front neck opening.

The pattern for making this shirt is in the section under men's clothing

18th Century Shirt Fabrics

As superintendent of the fur trade in 1755, William Johnson received consistent requests for "lively colors" in calicoes, ribbons and gartering from female Indians and children's shirts were often made in the same manner of the women, being somewhat smaller in size than the shirts made for the men. During the 18th century, ten pieces of garlix, a linen cloth imported from the Germanies, of three-fourths size, were ordered to make shirts for children of different ages (*Jacobs* 1967: p. 47).

In 1796, a wife of a Mohawk sachem received two and one-half yards of linen or calico (for a shirt), a plain hat, and two silk handkerchiefs. These were to be used with gifts consisting of five yards of cloth for a blanket and petticoat, thirty-six yards of ribbons, and 200 brooches. (*Jacobs* 1967: pp. 47-48)

(The following fabrics came from those listed among the William Johnson papers of the French and Indian War Period.)

Cotton calicoes

Calliminicoes - A wool product, woven with satin twill, enabling the observer to see checks on one side only. Indian agents ordered this glossy material in stripes and lively colors.

Walsh Cotton - A kind of woolen cloth with a nap.

Linen - In plain and printed (resist dying).

All of these fabrics were dyed bright hues of red, blue, and aurora in order to make them attractive to the Indians (*Jacobs* 1967: p. 51).

By the 13th century, an efficient and extensive textile industry had been developed in France. Dyes used there until the 18th century were saffron, woad, madder, kermes, walnut root, alder bark, oak bark, yellow-wood, gallnuts and vitriol. The French also increased the dyer's craft by developing varied dyeing techniques to achieve additional colors from the basic dyestuffs. By 1600, 220 master dyers were listed in Paris alone.

The great advance in dyeing methods began in France in the 18th century, when a dye chemistry based on scientific principles was developed. Natural dyes were universally used until the late 1800s, when aniline dye began to appear (*Brooklyn Botanic Gardens* 1984: p. 8).

In the printing of calico, a technique called resist dyeing was used. This is a preparation applied to parts of the fabric that was not to be colored, in order to prevent the color from fixing. It was employed when a pattern of small light motifs was desired on a large dark background in one color and the effect was produced by coating the portion of the fabric to be left white with wax or clay. The entire fabric was then dyed. Wherever the coating had been applied, the fabric "resisted" penetration of the dye and upon removal of the wax, a white pattern was left on the dark background.

Fabrics imported into the Indian trade in this country in many ways reflected the cultures of the countries that provided them:

French Textiles: "To the reign of Louis XV belong all the romantic frivolities that took such a hold on the French people of the eighteenth century. Never have more beautiful silks been made, with more intricacy of weave. Lace motifs grew in popularity and did, indeed, provide a suitable background for the playful patterns. Long streamers of ribbon were entwined with cupids and turtledoves in asymmetrical designs with scrolls and abundant flowers. Importation from the Far East set the vogue for the adaptation of Chinese patterns, known as *chinoiseries*, which were so typical of this era. Everything was light and dainty in scale, color, and texture, and the curved line dominated all design.

"A reversal of style occurred in the third quarter of the century, when the neoclassical forms were introduced as a result of the excavation of Pompey. The curves were replaced by straight lines. Stripes were over-patterned with fragile little bouquets of flowers in natural colorings."

English Textiles: "To understand the chintzes, hand-blocked lines, and crewel embroideries which England has become known for producing, it is necessary to go back to the early days of cotton in India. It is from India that England borrowed techniques and patterns. Indian and cotton have gone hand in hand from as early as 2000 B.C., though no actual pieces of cloth of that period are in existence. Cotton was not woven to any great extent in England until the thirteenth century. At about the same time, the merchants of India began to export their bright chintzes, first to the ports of Venice, and finally to Portugal. From there, the traders carried them to France, England and America.

"The printed cottons caught the fancy of the English, and they tried in vain to reproduce them. They soon discovered it was simpler to send their designs to India and have them made there. In the seventeenth and eighteenth centuries, rival trading companies brought in such quantities of printed cotton that both England and France decided to protect the home industry by excluding the "indiennes,: as they were often called. The first large cotton mill was set up in Manchester, England in the early part of the eighteenth century.

"By the end of the eighteenth century, Indian patterns were out of style, and England was making designs that were distinctly adapted to cotton. The large central floral spray was, of course, derived from the original Indian pattern, but the flowers were truly English. Porcelain motifs copied from real porcelains came into vogue, and later, with the revived interest in classicism, many classical motifs were included.

"The English patterns of the early nineteenth century were not so ostentatious as the French, though a definite relationship between the two was apparent. Realism in pattern design was brought to the fore, but England's chintzes and hand-blocked linens were far more outstanding than any of its woven fabrics." (*Whiton*, 1974: pp. 541-546)

FIGURE 19
18th Century Floral Chintz Shirt Fabrics

INDIAN WOMAN - 18th CENTURY

In the early days of the fur trade, Indian women received calico or linen trade shirts. The fabric was from India or England where they tried to imitate the brilliant India prints. The shirts were given as part of the gift giving policy of the superintendent of the fur trade. The shirts, when worn by the women, were worn for special occasions in the early 18th century. Later in the century, the shirt was nearly always worn as part of the woman's ensemble. The shirt was often decorated with silver brooches of various sizes, trade beads were worn in multiple layers around the neck and finger-woven sashes added color and shape when worn around the waist. These shirts were worn by women from the eastern Pennsylvania Delaware to the Huron of Quebec, the Shawnee and Miami of Ohio and Indiana as well as the Indian women living in parts of Wisconsin, Illinois and Minnesota.

Hair - Tied back in club fashion behind the nape of the neck

Silver Ear Wheels - One (1) in each ear

Calico Trade Shirt - Cotton or linen fabrics with large Indian prints

Silver Ring Brooches - Worn on the shoulders; and larger cut brooches worn on the lower front and hem of the shirt

Trade Bead Necklaces - These, along with a silver cross of Lorraine, worn around the neck

Blanket or *Matchcoat* - Worn over the shirt

Wrap-Around Skirt - Made of wool duffle or stroud and decorated with silk ribbon or wool braid trim on hem and silver ring brooches in diamond patterns just above the hem - Petticoat made of cotton, chintz, silk or linen could be worn instead

Leggings - From wool stroud with wings decorated with two colors of silk ribbon running parallel on wing edge and around the ankles

Moccasins - center seam, one-piece moccasins with ears or wing flaps decorated with two colors of silk ribbons

FIGURE 20

FIGURE 20

By the 1820s many of the Indian women were observed wearing a caped shirt or blouse embellished with many silver brooches over a petticoat trimmed in ribbons of various colors. An English artist named George Winter came to Indiana in 1837 and made a pictorial record of the Miami and Potawatomi Indians living along the Wabash and Eel rivers. Winter describes the "toute ensemble" of Frances Slocum, a captive living among the Miami in the following manner: "She was dressed in red calico shirt figured with large showy yellow and green folded within the upper part of her metacoshe or petticoat of black cloth of excellent quality. Her nether limbs were clothed with fady-red leggins, winged with green ribbons, and her feet were moccasinless." (*Winter* 1948: p. 176)

The caped shirt that was worn by the Huron of Quebec as well as the Miami, Shawnee, Potawatomi, Menominee and Illini tribes was based in part on a European drop sleeve trade shirt. As with that particular style, the shirt was composed of a loosely fitted bodice reaching to the abdomen and often covering the hips. These had long blousy sleeves, with a fitted cuff that buttoned or tied at the wrist with a ruffle over each hand. The women added a large over-the-shoulder cape-like collar that shows up in many forms in museum collections and paintings (*Winter* 1948: Plates IX, XIV, XVIII, XIX).

Some capes consisted of one large ruffle draped over the shoulders with a one to three inch secondary ruffle sewn to the bottom of the first. Others were modified further with an almost V-shaped yoke that formed the nucleus of the cape to which long pieces of fabric were sewn. At the neck opening, a smaller piece of fabric was gathered and stitched forming a fold-over collar (*Cranbrook* #2212). Other variations included several ruffles stitched together lengthwise and gathered to a circular neck band that was in turn stitched to the neck opening. The sizes of the ruffles varied greatly even among members of the same tribe (*Indiana History Bulletin* 1966: pp. 132-135). The ruffle edges appear to have remained plain until ribbon was used in the mid-19th century (*Conn* 1975: p. 71). Cuff ruffles ranged in width from one to two inches and were attached by folding tiny pleats of the ruffle (instead of gathering it) and hand-stitching it into the cuffs.

The origin of the shirt with large cape is not clear. It is likely that they developed from a similar style seen in men's hunting frocks. Hunting frocks worn by Indian men and caped-shirts of similar style worn by Indian women were worn frequently after the Revolutionary War (*Harrington* 1987: Personal Interview).

Shirt embellishment was very important to the Indian women. Silver brooches of varying sizes were used on the capes of the shirt and placed in several rows around the front and the back. The wearing of large numbers of brooches on the bodice was fashionable, quantity being a measure of status and wealth.

SHIRT WITH CAPE 1780-1845

Several variations of this caped blouse or shirt began to appear in paintings and journals from the Huron at Quebec to the Miami and Potawatomi of Indiana and Michigan. The Menominee of Wisconsin and the Shawnee of Ohio also wore a similar style. Several variations of the shirt with cape are shown below.

Materials needed: 4 yards of 45" linen, cotton, or chintz in either plain or block print.

1 - Construction: Make body of shirt based on the 18th century style shirt (See the section on *Men's Clothing* for the complete pattern).

2 - Cape Construction: Cut 3 pieces that are 6" wide by 15" long and sew the three pieces together forming a ruffle that is 45" in length. Then,

3 - Cut 4 pieces that are 4" wide by 15" long for the bottom ruffle and sew the four pieces together forming a ruffle that is 60" in length. Gather the 60" ruffle to fit the 45" ruffle and sew together forming a 9" long cape.

Gather the top of the ruffle to fit neck edge of shirt and pin and sew.

Options: Ruffles forming cape may be of any size combination or a third ruffle can be added for more fullness. Variations of the shirt with cape are seen throughout the George Winter Paintings of the 1830s and from museum pieces in the Heye Foundation in New York, the Milwaukee Public Museum, Chicago Field Museum, Cranbrook Institute and the Detroit Public Museum to name a few.

Another option is to add a half-circle yoke to the back of the cape center.

Using the Basic 18th Century Man's Shirt Pattern, you may use these variations: (**1**) No fold-over collar (optional), (**2**) Use a round neckline, (**3**) Add cape with a 4" yoke, and (**4**) an optional stand-up or fold-over collar with the addition of a detachable cape tied in the front with ribbon.

FIGURE 21 -DELAWARE STYLE BLOUSE

Open Front Cape with 4" Ruffle, Ribbon Trim and/or a Line of Brooches
Documented from an article written by Ty Stewart on Oklahoma Delaware Women's Dance Clothing based on interviews with Delaware
and Mrs. Nora Dean (Touching Leaves).

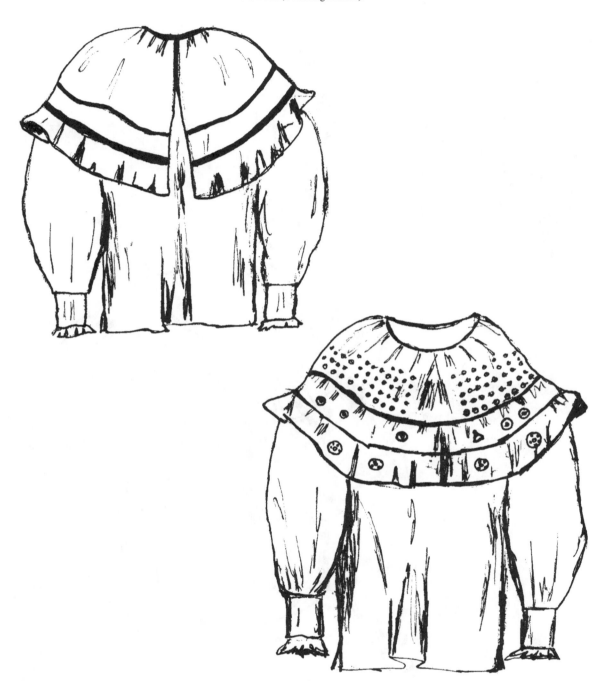

FIGURE 22 - POTAWATOMI STYLE BLOUSE

Yoke Style with Solid Front Cape featuring Brooches of all sizes and shapes.
Brooches were usually set in rows and blouses were often covered with silver brooches; sometimes with as many as 350 3/4" ring style
brooches arranged in 6-8 rows on the front and back of the cape.
Potawatomi Style from the George Winter Painting, 1837.
Based on an 1800s style POTAWATOMI BLOUSE in the Milwaukee Museum.
Made of red calico that is trimmed with black and green ribbon. (circa 1890)

FIGURE 23 & 24 - POTAWATOMI (Wisconsin)
- MENOMINEE STYLE BLOUSE (1820s)

from the *Denver Art Museum*. Made of calico with ribbon trim.
Although the ribbon shirt and blouse were made of European cloth and incorporated European ideas of clothing construction such as gathering, separate cuffs, gussets, etc., the simple binary cut maintained principles of native garments.

3½ - 4 yds. MATERIAL (45") 8 yds. — ⅜" RIBBON

Cut cape ruffle and sleeves first

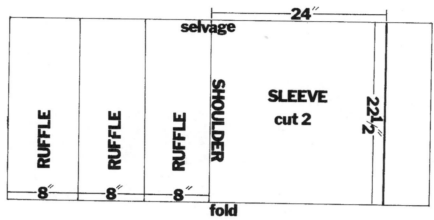

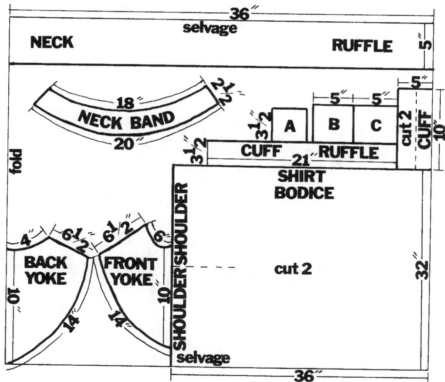

A: NECK
GUSSETS B: SLEEVE CUT 2 OF EACH
C: SIDE

FIGURE 25
CRANBROOK BLOUSE
Miami

This blouse is so named due to the fact that it is housed in the Cranbrook Institute in Bloomfield, Michigan just north of Detroit. The blouse was labeled *"Miami collected in Wabash County, Indiana, but with no date."*

Fabric suggestion: Linen, cotton or chintz in block print or plain color such as red, blue, yellow or black.

It will require 4 yards of 45" width fabric.

1 - To make this blouse, fold the fabric lengthwise and, with a ruler, measure off ruffle width (Ruffles - cut 3 that are 45" x 8"). Cut out and then cut sleeves.

2 - Then, open up the fabric and fold crossgrain. Lay out the body, cape, ruffle collar, cuffs and yoke. Cut and sew the body and sleeves - putting gussets in the proper places.

3 - In the construction of the yoke: (A) Sew the front of the yoke to the back at the shoulder seam; (B) Sew the cape ruffles seams and, with a narrow hem, the two short sides and one long side - you may add ribbon trim if desired; (C) Gather the remaining long side and pin it to the yoke while matching the ruffle seams to the x's on the yoke back; (D) Sew a 1/2" seam. Sew again 1/4" away from the seam and then trim close to the second seam; and (E) Sew ribbon along yoke and ruffle seam on the right side.

4 - Add the yoke to the bodice - mark the bodice, gather the neck edge and pin the yoke to the blouse. Make neck band and pin this on top of blouse and yoke. Sew - taking 1/2" seam - then turn the raw edge inside neckband and slipstitch down (like a sleeve cuff).

(Pattern by Colleen Antonides of Grand Rapids, Ohio.)

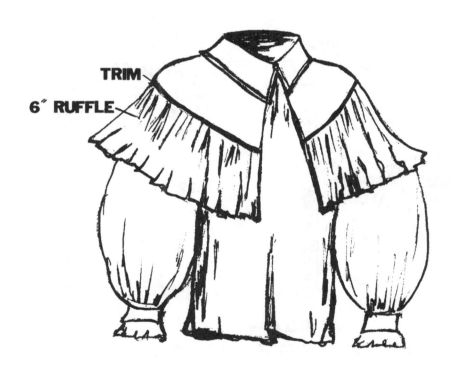

Original Miami Blouse - Found at Cranbrook Institute, Bloomfield Hills, Michigan
Circa 1830 - Wabash County, Indiana
Navy Blue - White dotted design; 3/4" Ring brooches front and back cape

TRIM

6" RUFFLE

FIGURE 26
CRANBROOK BLOUSE - FRONT

The pictorial record of the fur trade indicates that a chemise was sometimes worn with a wrap-around skirt. The chemise came into the hands of the Indian maiden perhaps due to the missionary influence or as a few necessary items added to basic trade lists. The Mackinaw Island State Park Commission has an anonymous drawing done in a very old style of an Indian woman wearing a chemise over a skirt (*Armour* 1972: pp. 76-77). Other references include Jonathan Carver's journal which includes an illustration of a 1760s Fox woman wearing what appears to be a chemise over a skirt. A later drawing done by Catherine Reynolds dated 1813 also shows a woman wearing a white chemise over a skirt and leggings at Fort Maiden (*American Heritage* 1982: p. 206).

Embellishment of the chemise is lacking the above-mention examples, but it is feasible that the chemise could have been decorated with silver brooches, necklaces, and a fingerwoven sash much in the same manner as with trade shirts.

A fitted jacket was also added to a woman's ensemble, worn over a chemise or trade shirt and wrap-around skirt. From an archaeological excavation conducted by the Oshkosh Public Museum, it was determined that a Menominee Indian woman was buried around 1780 wearing a dark green jacket with six large pewter buttons sewn to the front. She was also wearing a blue stroud skirt with white beads sewn in a zigzag near the bottom. Fabric from both the jacket and skirt was still visible when the remains were unearthed.

Another visual example of a jacket being worn by an Indian woman over a chemise was that of a Chip

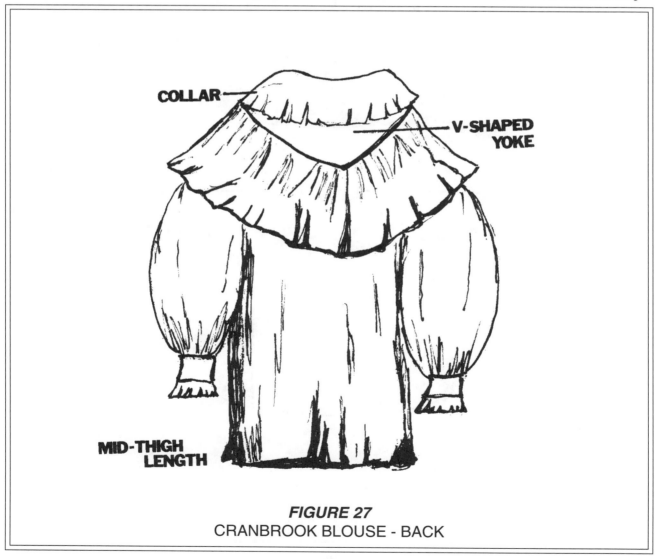

FIGURE 27
CRANBROOK BLOUSE - BACK

pewa woman who posed for a portrait by Charles Bird King in 1827. The jacket was made of red wool embellished with pale pink ribbon, blue ribbon, silver brooches, and three buttons held it closed in the front (*Horan* 1972: pp. 230-232).

A third example of a jacket or short gown was worn by Theresa Rankin, a Menominee woman, in her wedding of 1802. The fabric is a printed beige linen with ribbon or braid trim around the bottom edge and down each side of the front opening. The front was probably held together with hooks and eyes and was shorter in length than the back. The jacket was basically fitted to the waist and began to flare out over the hips as a triangular-shaped piece of matching fabric was inserted on each side.

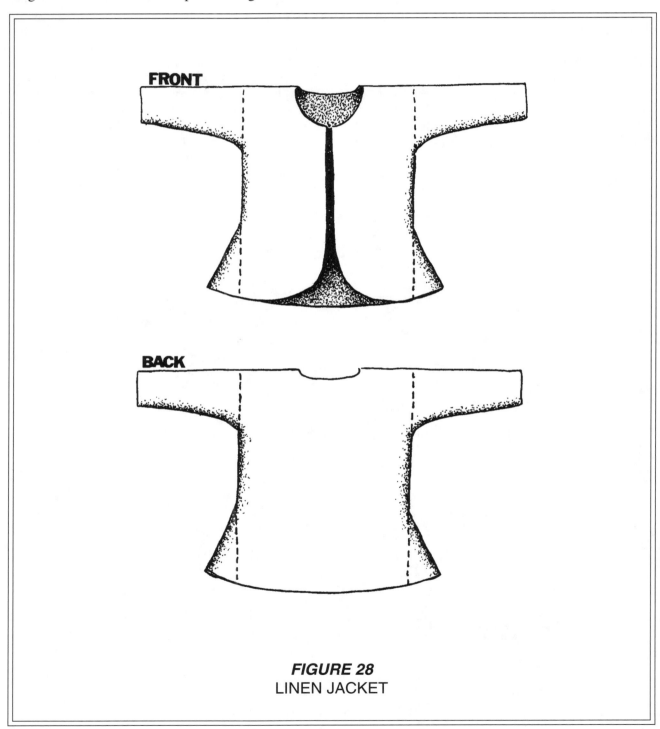

FIGURE 28
LINEN JACKET

FIGURE 29

As illustrated in *Figure 30*, the construction of a typical chemise will require 3 1/2 to 4 yards of unbleached muslin, cotton or linen gauze.

1 - Cut both layers of fabric at the first dotted line forming the back of the neckline

2 - Cut the top layer of fabric at the second dotted line, forming the front neckline

3 - Cut the body as indicated on the dotted line

4 - Place right sides together and stitch the triangular pieces to the straight sides of the body. Sew the side seams up to 12" from the top.

5 - Sleeves have a narrow fold-over hem at the wrist and casing made 2" above the wrist by running a 10" piece of bias tape on the wrong side of each sleeve. A hole is made at the seam to run the drawstrings through.

6 - Make the gussets. Sew to sleeves - stitch the sleeve seam from wrist to gusset. Gather the top of the sleeve and stitch to the body.

7 - With the wrong side of the bias tape to the right side of the neckline, start at the center front of the neck and pin bias tape to the edge and stitch.

8 - Press the tape to the inside of the body and hem in place. Insert 1 1/2 yards of twill tape for use as a drawstring at the neckline. Then hem the bottom of the body.

FIGURE 30

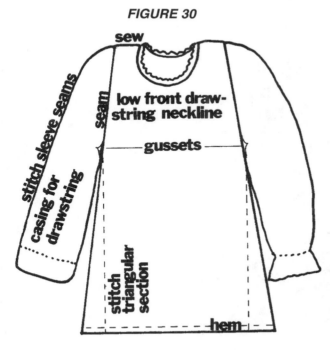

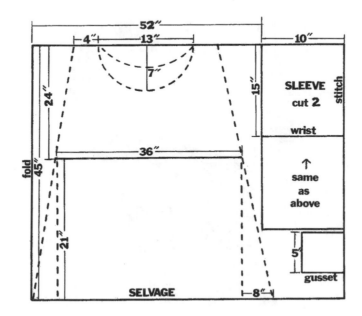

FIGURE 31

JACKET

In order to make the Jacket, it will require 2 1/2 to 3 yards of wool, linen or cotton broadcloth, 1 1/2 yards of bias tape and 3 yards of 1/2" ribbon.

1 - Cut the three jacket pieces as per the diagram

2 - Place the right sides together, stitch the front to the back at the shoulders, lower edges of sleeves and side seams

3 - Place a hole that is 1/2" long vertically in the center back and reinforce it with stitching at the waistline

4 - On the wrong side, run bias tape along the waistline from the front center edge to the center back hole. Stitch both edges to form the casing. Do the same on the other side.

5 - Start at the front and run a one yard long ribbon through each casing and out through the center back hole to the right side. Stitch the ribbon end and the casing along the front edge.

6 - Bind the raw edges with ribbons. Embellish with silver brooches, brass bells and buttons.

This style and variations thereof was worn by some Indian women over a chemise, blouse, or man's shirt with a wrap-around skirt. (*Source: McKenny-Hall Portrait Gallery; C.B. King artistic rendering, 1820s among the Chippewa.*)

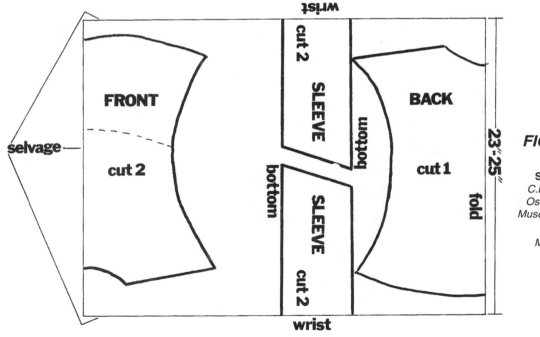

FRONT cut 2

selvage

wrist

SLEEVE cut 2

bottom

SLEEVE cut 2

bottom

wrist

BACK cut 1

23"-25"

fold

FIGURE 32

SOURCES:
*C.B. King 1827
Oshkosh Public
Museum Collection
1780*

Menominee

FIGURE 33

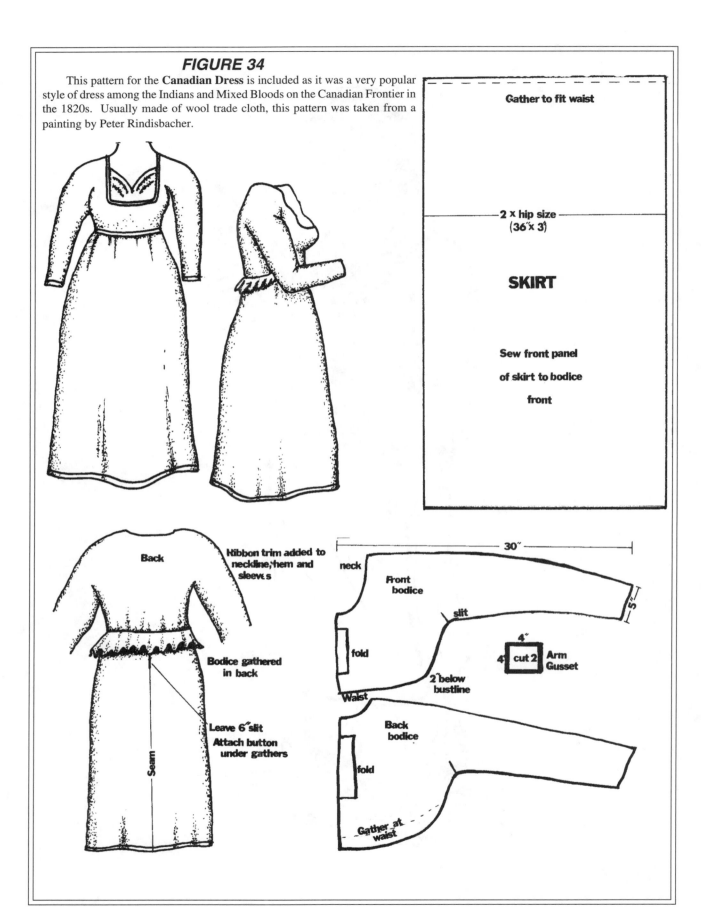

FIGURE 34

This pattern for the **Canadian Dress** is included as it was a very popular style of dress among the Indians and Mixed Bloods on the Canadian Frontier in the 1820s. Usually made of wool trade cloth, this pattern was taken from a painting by Peter Rindisbacher.

Gather to fit waist

2 × hip size
(36˝ × 3˝)

SKIRT

Sew front panel

of skirt to bodice

front

Back

Ribbon trim added to neckline, hem and sleeves

Bodice gathered in back

Leave 6˝ slit
Attach button under gathers

Seam

neck

Front bodice

slit

fold

Waist

2˝ below bustline

30˝

5˝

4˝
4˝ cut 2 Arm Gusset

Back bodice

fold

Gather at waist

Ribbons were used in the fur trade as "gifts" or "presents" to the Indians and as early as 1755 captive James Smith reported that the Indians "... gave me a new ruffled shirt, which I put on, also a pair of leggins done off with ribbons and beads ..." (*Ohio Historical Society* 1978: p. 30).

Rudimentary silk ribbonwork appears in paintings made in 1788 by British artillery officer Thomas Davies. At Point Levy near Quebec, Huron Indians are shown utilizing alternate colors of ribbon applied to blankets or matchcoats.

The use of ribbons again appears in 1762 as described by John Heckewelder. "Her scarlet leggings were decorated with different coloured ribands sewed on, the outer edge being finished off with small beads also of various colours." (*Wallace* 1985: p. 59)

Ribbonwork is a general term applied to the use of silk ribbons sewn to cloth for decorative purposes. There are several ways in which ribbons were applied to the cloth thus creating different visual effects. Early 19th century examples show several varieties on one garment. First, ribbon strips were laid in parallel rows leaving only a fraction of an inch between ribbons. The second method was to lay ribbons of one color on a background ribbon of another color in such a way as to form zigzag lines. Those ribbons on top were then folded under and stitched to the background ribbon. The third method was referred to as cut ribbon applique. In this method, ribbons of alternated colors are placed one on top of the other. A design was drawn on the top ribbon and cuts were made into the design and the loose fragments folded under and blind-stitched thus revealing the ribbon underneath as the actual design (*Neville Public Museum* # 70/1948).

To further complicate the issue of ribbonwork styles, Kathleen Abbass has divided ribbonwork applique into three construction techniques. *Type One* is plain applique which involves only a piece of cloth torn into a strip or cut into a simple shape and sewn down to a larger piece. *Type Two* is based upon a strip of cloth folded several times laterally, cut in a "half figure," and finally unfolded into a repeating design. Then it is appliqued on another piece of cloth. In most cases, *Type Two* applique is made in bands four inches wide or less and usually in curvilinear figures set bilaterally along a horizontal axis. *Type Three* applique is generally worked in rectilinear figures, but instead of being bilateral on a central axis, there will usually be a linear figure repeated two or more times. The most common form of this type is the geometric ribbonwork of the Great Lakes in the first half of the 19th century (*Horse Capture*

1980: pp. 9-10).

In *Type Three*, a series of ribbon strips was used, laid and cut to produce a series of triangles, diamonds, rhomboids, and rectilinear figures. Using this technique, great variety of design could be obtained. Triangles or diamonds might be continuous or joined by other figures of varying sizes and proportions. This was in duplication of a type of design often executed in woven or embroidered quillwork and it is known in many Great Lakes tribes as "otter tail" design.

To start *Type Three* technique, two ribbons were laid side by side on top of the background ribbon. One-half of the pattern is then traced on each ribbon so there was a mirror image on the opposite ribbon. These were then basted in place. Then, starting with the first section of the design, a cut was made into the design, thus allowing the ribbon to be folded under and blind-stitched in place. This method is carried out until all designs on both top ribbons have been cut and stitched in place. Only a little is done at a time to prevent slipping or fraying.

The background ribbon can be of the same size as two of the top ribbons or it can cover a larger area as alternate colors of ribbons are placed on top and stitched into place. The design can continue to grow laterally by stitching more rows of ribbons into place at pre-determined distances from each other, allowing the background ribbon to show in between. This was the technique used on the wedding garment ensemble of Theresa Rankin, now housed in the Neville Public Museum at Green Bay, Wisconsin, dated 1802 (*Horse Capture* 1980: p. 21).

Colors were often selected with care and feeling. Beyond aesthetic considerations, they might involve religious symbolism. For example, among the Menominee, colors were looked upon as protective emblems of the "Sky Women" (*Skinner* 1921). There were four "Celestial Sisters" in the southern sky who, with four in the east, controlled the destinies of women. Each of the southern sisters had the power to travel and befriend women in one of four directions. The colors for the directions were: red for east; black for north; white, yellow and blue for south and west; and, there is some confusion about the last colors used. (*Skinner* 1921).

Eric Douglas felt that the designs came from the quillwork and engraved birchbark containers. Alanson Skinner felt that the ribbonwork geometric designs have an origin in quillwork dating from the early 17th century. Skinner also felt that leather applique, though more rare, is a forerunner of ribbonwork (*Horse Capture* 1980: p. 19).

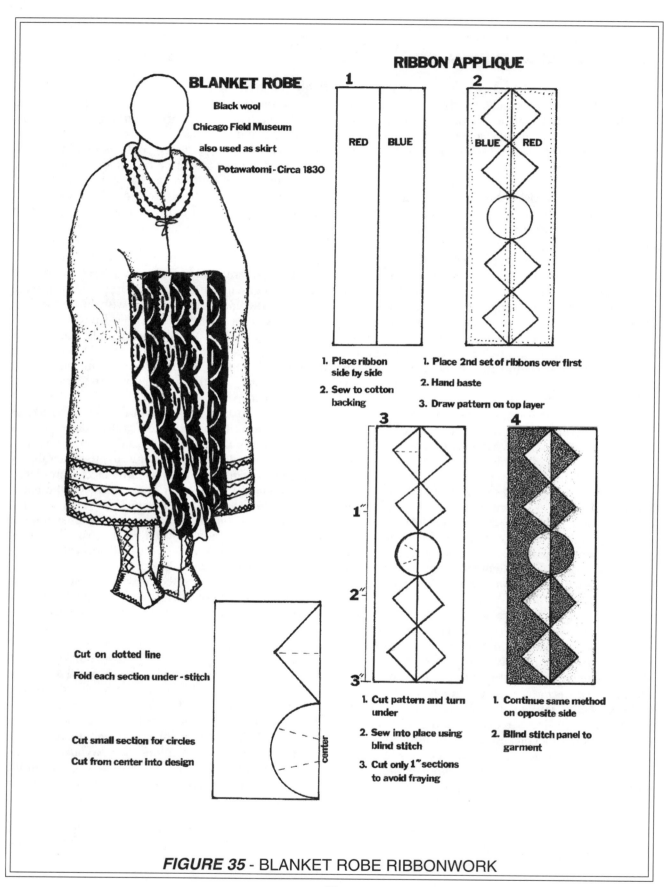

BLANKET ROBE

Black wool

Chicago Field Museum

also used as skirt

Potawatomi - Circa 1830

RIBBON APPLIQUE

1

RED   BLUE

2

BLUE   RED

1. Place ribbon side by side
2. Sew to cotton backing

1. Place 2nd set of ribbons over first
2. Hand baste
3. Draw pattern on top layer

3

1"

2"

3"

4

1. Cut pattern and turn under
2. Sew into place using blind stitch
3. Cut only 1" sections to avoid fraying

1. Continue same method on opposite side
2. Blind stitch panel to garment

Cut on dotted line

Fold each section under - stitch

Cut small section for circles

Cut from center into design

center

FIGURE 35 - BLANKET ROBE RIBBONWORK

Probably the most popular design of the Great Lakes region was the "Otter Tail" design (**Type Three**), said by the old women to represent the track left by the otter when it crosses the ice in the spring. The typical otter tail border consisted of narrow elongated hexagons with two, three or four diamonds connecting them, the vertical width of the hexagons and the diamonds being the same. The otter tail is an old weaving design and may have come to the Algonquin Indians from their eastern Iroquois neighbors (*Lyford* 1982: p. 144).

"Leaf designs" were used in many forms both natural or semi-realistic and conventionalized. Realistic maple, oak, and wild grape leaves all showing veins as well as outlines were popular as designs on birch bark baskets and later revised to fit the ribbon applique (*Lyford* 1982: p. 145).

In the early days of ribbon applique the Indian women would tear or cut out birch bark, rawhide or paper patterns for the floral motifs which they expected to use in their ribbonwork. An old bladder bag filled with patterns of leaves, roses, and other flowers is a treasure much prized by the collector and a woman will seldom part with her carefully collected patterns. They are among her most personal possessions; death is the only separation. A few well-filled bladder bags are found in museum collections.

Design varies with the tribe, but tribal identification of them is not a simple matter. Certain designs are not the exclusive property of one tribe. The same design may be shared by several tribes, the only difference being in the treatment of that design (*Neville Public Museum* #70/1948. Menominee: *Cranbrook Institute* #2208, Miami).

The area of highest ribbonwork development was the Great Lakes Region. Exactly where and when it actually began is still a matter of conjecture. Tribes that produced ribbonwork included Menominee, Miami, Shawnee, Delaware, Ottawa, Kickapoo, Winnebago, Piankeshaw, Huron, Illini, Sac, Fox, Huron, and Iroquois. A second area was to be found on the eastern Plains where tribes like the Osage, Iowa and Sisseton Sioux are generally considered to have been the most skillful, but the art was also practiced by the Oto, Kaw, Pawnee, Ponca, Omaha, Quawpaw, Caddo and Wichita. A third area of ribbonwork development, although weak, is in the Northeast of New England, New York and Eastern Canada. Tribes included the Mohegan, Penobscot, Narraganset, and some of the Iroquois. Finally, there is the southeast, where the art was not highly developed, but was practiced by such groups as the Cherokee, Choctaw, Chickasaw, Creek, Yuchi, Koasati, Alabamu, Catawba and Seminole (*Marriott*, 1958).

It is important to note that in many of the contem-

FIGURE 36
TYPE ONE APPLIQUE

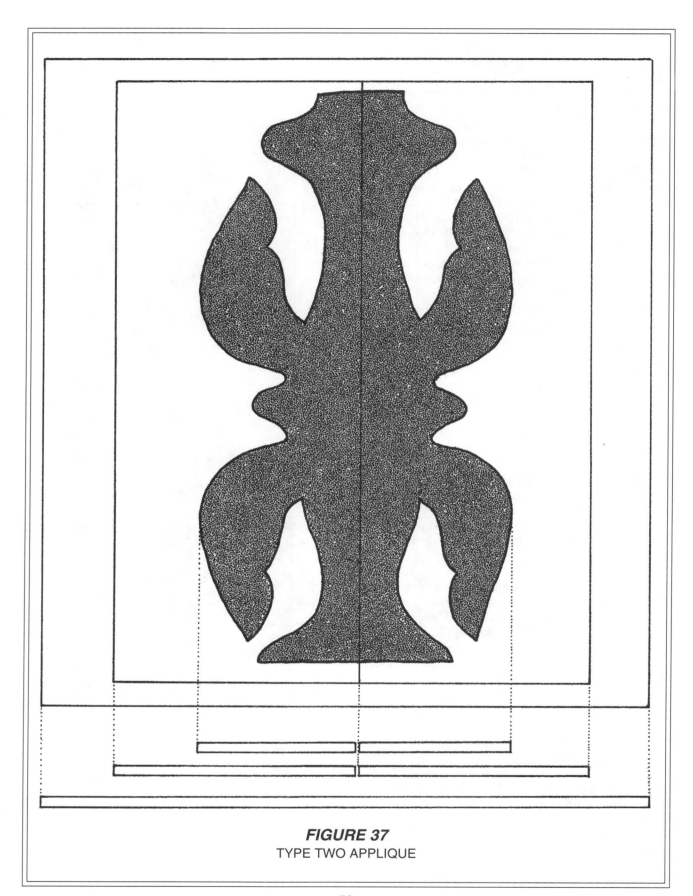

FIGURE 37
TYPE TWO APPLIQUE

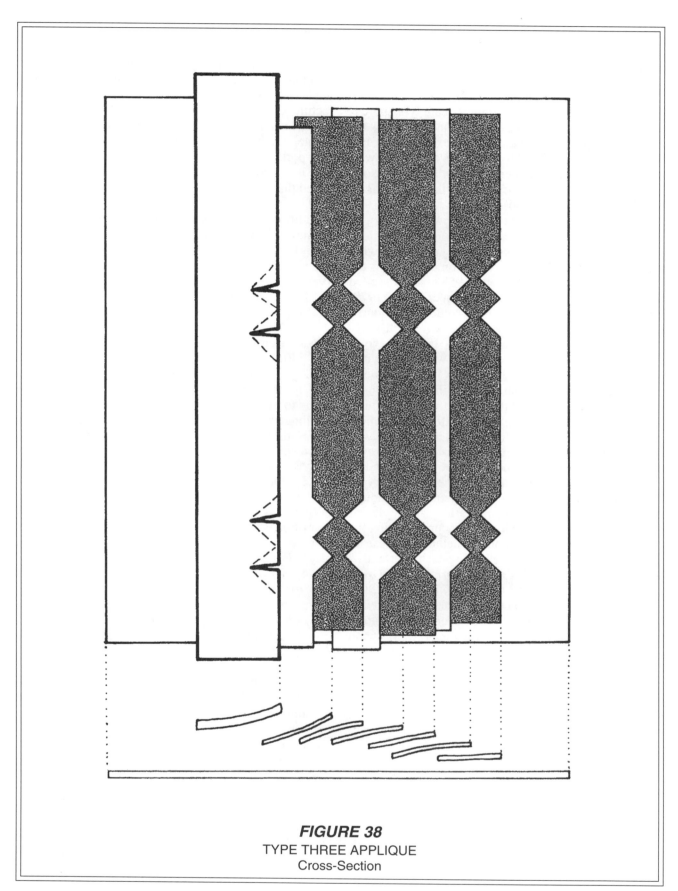

FIGURE 38
TYPE THREE APPLIQUE
Cross-Section

51

porary tribal groups listed above, craftspeople are still producing outstanding examples of the beautiful art form.

The applique technique seems to have its roots in pre-contact art traditions. Examples of applying porcupine quills and moose hair to leather and birchbark for examples found in archaeological excavations date from 1300 - 1400 A.D. More designs developed with the introduction of implements such as thread, scissors, needles and silk ribbons during the 18th century (*Skinner*, 1921 and *Feder*, 1956).

Several authors stated that ribbonwork developed when French ribbons were dumped on the American market because of regulations of luxury dress following the French Revolution; this has become known as the Dumping Hypothesis. Marriott's 1958 essay was cited in several articles claiming this influence (*Abbass* 1979; Brasser 1976, 1982). This claim is somewhat disputed by Rachael Pannabecker when she wrote: "Briefly stated, simplicity in dress following the French Revolution created stocks of merchandise which were disposed in the New World markets. This hypothesis explains an apparently greater availability of ribbons to the Great Lakes Indians at the end of the 18th century. Investigation of this theory yielded information which places this assumption of dumping in doubt.

"The effect of dress regulations issued by the revolutionary assembly of France has not been named as contributing to problems in the ribbon industry in histories of French ribbon manufacture. Although changes in the fabrics, ornamentation, and styles of French dress have been claimed to occur following the revolution it has been questioned whether legal restrictions were ever effective in halting fashion trends." (Rachael Pannabecker's "*Ribbonwork of the Great Lakes Indians: The Material of Acculturation*," 1986).

Even though European fashion had been moving toward simplified styles before the French Revolution, ribbons remained in common use for drawstrings on clothing and as bows and ties on caps and bonnets. And, since ribbons remained a part of the trimming industry rather than the silk fabric textile industry, manufacture of silk ribbon was not only affected by the fashion industry but also by sumptuary laws, natural disasters in production of silk fiber, and economic instability created by the financial demands of military clashes (*Pannabecker* 1986).

Pannabecker also points out that the dumping hypothesis ignores crucial facts about the North American market. The French defeat in 1760 all but eliminated commerce with France and, although the British maintained Montreal-Great Lakes trade routes and personnel, material goods were procured from suppliers in London. From 1768 to 1826 the importation of French ribbons into England was prohibited by the law. Thus the flow of ribbon to North America from France via London would have been curbed. Another point to be made is that England was as proficient in ribbon manufacture as France (*Pannabecker* 1986).

"Furthermore the type of ribbon produced in greater quantity was the "flowered" and thus a significant portion of French ribbon would not have been the type received by the Great Lakes Indians. It can also be stated that the ribbon industry about Coventry in England specialized in the manufacture of plain ribbon and in addition, the introduction of the "Dutch engine loom" around 1770 mechanized the fabrication of plain ribbon. The power loom allowed for quantity production not yet attainable in figured ribbons." (*Pannabecker* 1986).

It is interesting to note that there are many references to silk ribbon listed as trade goods. For example:

1 - 1755 William Johnson includes ribbons on goods listed for Indian gifts (*Johnson Papers*, I: pp. 539-540).

2 - On a dated list of presents to be made to the Mohawk Indians, the Wisconsin Historical Collection refers to the 1796-1797 period. According to this list, a Mohawk Chief's lady was to have, among other things, thirty-six yards of ribbon, two hundred brooches and a smaller blanket of only two and one-half points (*Jacobs* 1967: p. 48).

3 - John Johnson's Account Book 1802-1811 includes a variety of articles of adornment including types of ribbon available; China ribbon, assorted ribbon and hair ribbons. The China ribbon was valued at $ .60 per piece, and the other ribbon at $2.65, $3.00 and $3.30 per piece (*Pannabecker* 1986).

4 - The Menard and Valled Account Book which was for the Miami, Delaware and Shawnee Indians discusses ribbon selection. Five women were specifically mentioned as receiving ribbon in trade. In addition, 18 accounts of goods requested included the notation "*pr s/ femme*," "*a s/femme*," or variations thereof. (Translation: for his wife and to his wife), and "*pr sa niece*" (for his niece). Although the names on the account are Indian, it can be assumed that many of these accounts were for men, and that by the notation the trader was specifying the woman's role in the selection process or the woman as the exclusive recipient of the trade items. Nine of the 19 notations were for the specific purchase of ribbon (*Pannabecker* 1986).

5 - The Tardiveau Document - Memorandum concerning commerce with different "savage nations" written at the Ohio Falls in March 1784 - consisted of a nine page history of the Shawnee, Chickasaw, Choctaw, and Creek tribes (in French), followed by a nine page table (in English), regarding the types, colors, qualities, and saleability of each trade item for those tribes. Regarding ribbon, Tardiveau specified:

Plain, or of one colour, and very lively
2 yard for 1 skin
Deep and light reds, saxon & deep greens, deep and light blue, borad
yellows &. a few fllour'd wou'd likewise sell; half sattin ribbon call'd
Pealing better for the Southward. (*Pannabecker* 1986).

THE USE OF RIBBON IN THE 18TH CENTURY

Ribbon and other European textiles were selected by the Great Lakes Indians and incorporated into their native material culture. Great Lakes Indians used ribbon as clothing ornamentation as did Europeans, but modified its use in a uniquely non-European manner.

According to Reverend Father Nau, a Jesuit missionary in 1735, ribbons were noted to be used on a Chaughnawaga Indians' leggings. Chippewa and Huron chiefs were specifically listed as receiving wool blankets or strouds ornamented with ribbon from the British Indian Department in 1773 (*Sterling Papers*). Kalm writes more specifically of ribbons "...they have a short blue petticoat, which reaches to their knees and the brim of which is bordered with red or other ribbons..."

O.M. Spencer speaking of the Ohio Indians in the French and Indian War Period notes..." the borders of their leggings, and the bottom and edges of their strouds tastefully bound with ribands, edged with beads of various colors ..." Heckewelder, who explored the Ohio country also during this time notes that the "... women, at the expense of their husbands or lovers, line their petticoat with blue or scarlet cloth blanket or covering with choice ribands of various colours, or with gartering on which they fix a number of silver brooches, or small round buckles. They adorn the leggins in the same manner..." (*Pannabecker* 1986).

Beginnings of Ribbonwork

While no documented specimens of ribbonwork or ribbon decorated clothing from the 18th century are known to exist, verbal descriptions are corroborated by pictorial evidence of contrasting borders on garments. A mid-18th century portrait of a Huron couple from Lorette, who moved to Montreal after the Iroquois wars, depicts a woman wearing a dark-colored skirt with a contrasting light-colored band parallel and close to the bottom edge. The Huron man is portrayed wearing a dark robe with six light-colored bands placed edge to edge horizontally from the bottom hem of the robe (*Trigger* 1978: pp. 390-391). Similarly, an engraving of a Wyandot woman before 1772 shows her skirt with multiple horizontal bands.

Although there are no surviving examples of ribbonwork from the 18th century known to exist, an intricate style of ribbonwork dated 1802 is housed in the collections of the Neville Public Museum in Green Bay, Wisconsin. This example consists of a woman's robe, skirt, and leggings reputed to have been the wedding costume worn by Sophie Theresa Rankin of Menominee and French heritage, upon her marriage to Green Bay trader Louis Grignon in 1802.

The Rankin ensemble links the use of plain ribbon borders to cut and sewn ribbonwork. Of the decoration on the robe and skirt, more space is given to plain ribbon than ribbonwork. Multiple bands of wide ribbon parallel the bottom edges of the robe and skirt.

A structural type not identified in the Abbass typology (1979) is found on both the robe and skirt. Two colors of ribbon were applied to a third wide ribbon in a continuing criss-cross pattern. This double zig-zag resulting in a chain of diamond outlines appears on one strip on both vertical edges of the robe front, and on three strips on each vertical edge of the wrapped skirt front.

There are a number of ribbon applique examples that survive from the first quarter of the 19th century but few with written documentation. The Jasper Grant collection from the 1800-1809 period includes leggings, garter pendants, and moccasins and is from the National Museum of Ireland which was on display with other American Indian artifacts from Canadian museums in 1984 and 1985 in Canada. It simply lacks specific dates and tribal provenance although they were collected when Grant was posted at Fort George in the Niagara region and Fort Malden across from Detroit in 1800-1809.

Mrs. Baird's recollection of an 1819 wedding at Michilimachinac was not written down until late in the 19th century although it has been praised by editor R. G. Thwaites as accurate for the time and circumstances. Baird described plain ribbon borders and ribbon "embroidery" on the outfit worn by a full-blooded Indian bride marrying an American from Philadelphia:

"The skirt reached about half-way between the ankle and the knee, and was elaborately embroidered with ribbon and beads on both the lower and upper edges ... Above this horizontal trimming were rows upon rows of ribbons, four or five inches wide, placed so near together that only a narrow strip of cloth showed like a narrow cord. Accompanying this was worn a pair of leggings made of broadcloth ... the embroidery about three inches from the side edge. Around the bottom the

SILK RIBBON APPLIQUE

The *Rankin Ensemble* is the earliest dated remaining example of silk ribbon applique and may be seen in the Neville Public Museum in Green Bay, Wisconsin. This wedding dress and shawl belonged to Sophie Theresa Rankin, a Menominee woman. The intricate applique on the sides and hem of the skirt and shawl is combined with two inch silk ribbons placed horizontally, a fraction of an inch apart, creating a skirt almost entirely covered with ribbons, revealing little of the wool beneath. The ensemble illustrated three techniques of ribbon-work: Solid strips of Ribbon, Folded Ribbons and Cut-Work Applique.

The wedding took place in 1802 and the style is a Type Three applique described in more detail above. According to Rachael Pannabecker, who researched this piece thoroughly, the attendants at the wedding had similar outfits as well, all being finely developed silk applique skirts.

The outfit is worn in the following manner according to Dr. Nancy O. Lurie of the Milwaukee Public Museum and is currently pictured in this manner.

SHIRT - Variation of a jacket or short gown made of beige colored linen with a reddish block print design, edged with braid or ribbon in a deep red tone

SKIRT - The wool skirt is wrapped around the waist and gathered by hand and held in place with a wool sash. The ribbon applique panels that match are placed on the left side of the body and pinned in place. The skirt reached half-way between knee and ankle. The wool was blue

SHAWL - The shawl similarly decorated is not worn, but instead draped over one arm and carried with ribbonwork facing outward. The wool was bright red with blue, red, yellow and white ribbons

LEGGINGS - Wool sewn into a tube and fitted to leg with ribbon applique wing flap and hem

NOTE - *This ensemble has been pictured in a number of publications showing the skirt wrapped around the body with the ribbon applique center front and the top half of the skirt pulled over the upper half of the body. It also has been featured with the shawl draped over the head as a cape. Dr. Lurie has determined this to be a misrepresentation of the correct way in which this ensemble was worn. This is the first publication to feature the entire ensemble correctly worn. This outfit was personally examined by the author in 1987.*

FIGURE 39

FIGURE 39

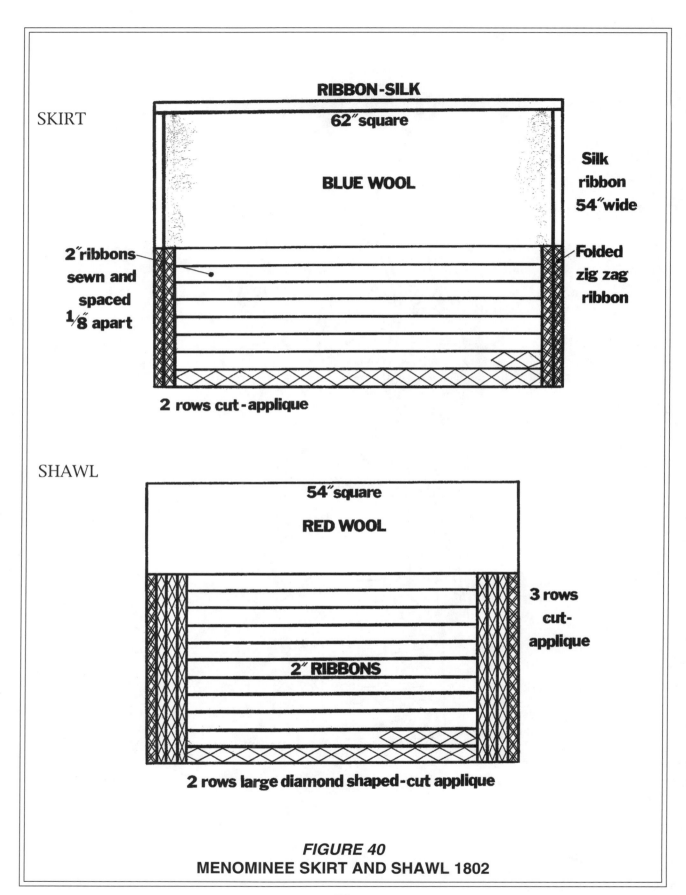

RIBBON-SILK

SKIRT

62″square

BLUE WOOL

Silk
ribbon
54″wide

2″ribbons
sewn and
spaced
⅛″ apart

Folded
zig zag
ribbon

2 rows cut-applique

SHAWL

54″square

RED WOOL

3 rows
cut-
applique

2″ RIBBONS

2 rows large diamond shaped-cut applique

FIGURE 40
MENOMINEE SKIRT AND SHAWL 1802

trimming is between four and five inches in width. The moccasins, also, were embroidered with ribbon and beads. Then we come to the blanket ... with most elaborate work of ribbon; no beads, however are used on it."

Baird also noted that similar ensembles were worn by the bride's Indian mother, and two women traders of French and Ottawa extractions, Theresa Schindler and Marie La Fremboise. While Baird did not clearly identify the construction techniques used in doing the ribbon embroidery, her description coincides closely to the Rankin garments illustrated in this book (*Pannabecker* 1986).

Evidence of Ribbonwork in the 1830s

Two portraits from the 1830s George Catlin collection provide visual documentation that silk applique had made its way into the eastern plains and prairies. A full-length portrait of Nahweerecoo the wife of Keokuk, a Sauk Indian, was painted in 1835. Wide bands of ribbonwork are clearly evident at the horizontal hem and left vertical front of the wrapped skirt. The horizontal piece contains multiple rows of equilateral diamonds common in shingled work. A second painting shows two Menominee men sketched at Prairie du Chien in 1835 or at Green Bay in 1836 wearing blankets bordered with silk ribbon-applique (*Hassrick* 1981: pp. 62, 87).

George Winter gives the first written detailed description of ribbonwork in Indiana use by Miami and Potawatomi Indians (1837-1839). He also painted many portraits of the Indians wearing such garments with ribbon-applique borders. In his published journal, Winter made various references to ribbon used on clothing: "Their leggins (Potawatomi) are made like ladies pantalettes but the cloth, and are adorned with wings, or wide side stripes handsomely adorned with many coloured ribbons..." "Her nether limbs were clothed with fady red leggins, 'winged' with green ribbons...her blanket and petticoat were of good dark blue broadcloth, handsomely bordered with ribbons..."

Winter also refers specifically to ribbonwork. "Their nether garments were also made of cloth, handsomely bordered with many coloured ribbons, shaped into singular forms..." "Her wrapper or otherwise petticoat is handsomely checkered by various coloured ribbons etc..." "Two or three pairs of 'leggins' with handsome borders, or 'wings' decorated with the primitive coloured ribbons, some sewed in diamond forms, others in straight lines..."

Some of Winter's paintings were published with selections of his journal in 1948 by the Indiana Historical Society. Clearly, Winter perceived the materials of Indian garments and ornamentation, including ribbon, to represent a significant use of economic resources. His reflections also constitute the earliest recognition of the amount of time and artistic creativity involved in ribbonwork (*Winter* 1948: pp. 137, 173, 176).

From a history of the state of Indiana published in 1889 comes a description of Miami clothing from Thomas Roche who worked with Chief Francis LaFontaine in the 1830s and 1840s. "On such occasions as the adoption dance...the young Indian fops would appear in their best, which was usually a frock coat with vest to match, leggings, upon which some artistic woman had spent many an hour to ornament in diamonds, stripes and blocks of ribbon work with the edges trimmed with beads. This ornamental work was always upon the flap or seam ... moccasins were the proper thing, trimmed to match the leggings."

Some additional visual documentation of ribbonwork are:

1780 circa painting of Sir John Caldwell which shows silk ribbons of one color that form row after row of embellishments on his matchcoat (*Brasser* 1976: Front Cover).

1788 painting of Quebec Indians by British officer Thomas Davies shows alternate colors of ribbons on the lower edge of a woman's skirt and two matchcoats or blankets (*Hassrick* 1981: p. 24).

1814 painting of two Ottawa by Sir Joshua Jebb in the Peabody Museum showing ribbons on leggings (*Fredrickson* 1980: p. 111).

1830 leggings with cut applique belonging to Francis Slocum, a Miami captive (*Ewing* 1982: p. 192).

1834 Juahkisgaw-Ojibwa woman holding cradleboard with ribbonwork wrapping (*Fredrickson* 1980: p. 147).

There also exist a number of undated surviving examples of ribbonwork in many regional museums. Among these are:

Miami woman's shawl or skirt with a collection date of 1860 (*Cranbrook Institute* #2208).

Miami woman's shawl or skirt with a collection date of 1840 (*Wabash County Museum*).

Potawatomi or Miami stroud cloth skirt or shawl, circa 1800 (*Denver Art Museum* #APw-1).

PATTERNS AND TECHNIQUES

Patterns, consisting of a single unit of design, were often saved for generations. These were primarily made of paper or birchbark (*Skinner*). Most of the work was done beforehand on light cotton material such as calico, and the finished strip was applied to the garment. Sometimes, where small diamond designs were used, especially on smaller garments or blankets, the design

FIGURE 41, 42 & 43 - WRAP SKIRT

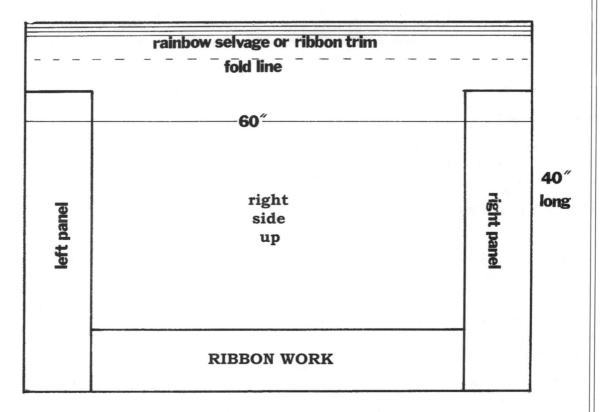

rainbow selvage or ribbon trim

fold line

60″

40″ long

left panel

right side up

right panel

RIBBON WORK

Ribbon panel side overlap

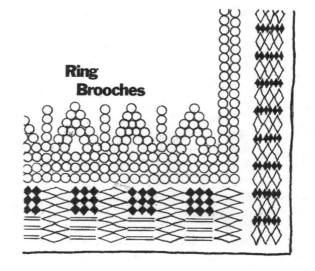

Ring Brooches

MIAMI SKIRT –
Cranbrook Institute

was applied directly and without backing.

First, for the process of planning designs and reading from left to right in the series of sketches shown below (*Figure 46*), the first step is to draw a line on a piece of paper about one inch wide. This line should consist of a series of pointed peaks based on the outline of connecting otter tail designs. Repeat this series for the length of your fabric. In this sketch, each side of the line is numbered 1 and 2. Now, cut the fabric along the line and reverse the pieces marked 1 (shown as 1r). Always begin this type of ribbonwork with a straight ribbon as shown in the second sketch.

The remaining sketches show how the design is built up using only your two basic patterns 1r and 2, and alternating first one and then the other until the finished design shown on the far right is formed. This example is shown using seven ribbons, but any odd number of ribbons may be used. This is so that you will always have a center ribbon to balance your design. Any color ribbon of the period may be used, but the first and last are usually the same color, the second and next to last are the same, etc. and the middle usually stands out in contrast.

The five designs shown in *Figure 47A* through *47E* are all variations of the same two basic patterns developed in *Figure 46*. Here, however, instead of alternating first one and then the other, we have changed the order and entirely different patterns result. Each of these patterns have the usual 13 ribbons.

From communications with Dr. Nancy O. Lurie of The Milwaukee Public Museum, I have learned that Kathleen Abbass has worked with their extensive collection of ribbonwork clothing in making further studies of it for later publications. Much of the clothing that I have personally examined is in very delicate condition and hence much of it will never be publically displayed or handled by future researchers. Both the Field Museum of Natural History in Chicago and the Milwaukee Public Museum are trying to find ways to preserve and protect what few examples remain of this material. SH

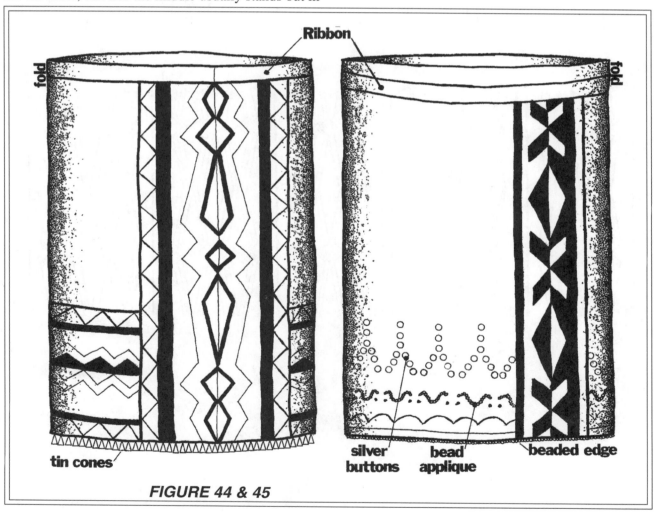

FIGURE 44 & 45

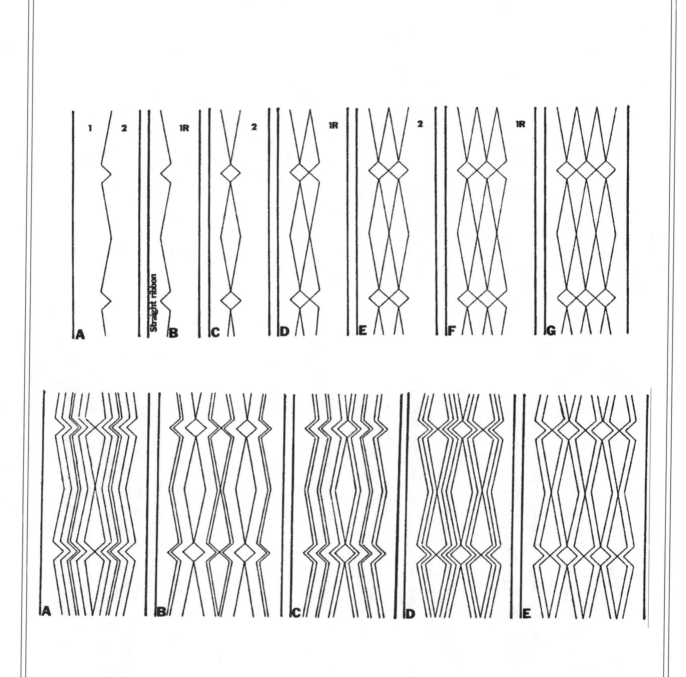

FIGURE 46 AND 47

silver buttons

2" center →

beaded edge

TRAILER RIBBONS

5"

FIGURE 48

The hairbow was worn by women in the Great Lakes Indian villages and has been used by Indian women from as far away as the Apache villages of the Southwest. It appears as early as the 17th century among the Huron women of Canada and much evidence indicates that it was still being used by Indian women in the Great Lakes right up through the removal period in the 1830s and 1840s.

Of those found in museum collections, the hairbows were made from an hourglass-shaped rawhide base covered with leather or cloth and decorated with silver or brass buttons or brooches. Ribbon ties were attached and left hanging down the back, often 36" to 50" in length.

A typical Hairbow may be constructed using the following instructions:

1 - From heavy leather, rawhide or heavy cardboard, cut out an hourglass shape that measures 4" wide at the top, tapering it 4" down so that the center measures 2" across and then tapering up 4" so that the bottom (the base) measures 5" wide.

2 - Cut out an hourglass-shaped covering consisting of two pieces of wool or leather (black, blue, red or brown) with the same dimensions as the above plus 1/2" to 3/4" seam allowance all the way around. This will form the cover.

3 - Sew both ends and one side of the covering together at the right sides.

4 - Turn so that the right sides of the cover are out and insert the base. Then hand-stitch the remaining side closed by turning the raw edges inside.

5 - Decorate all of the seams with edge beading, using white 8/° pony beads or 10/° seed beads. Old pieces show a 1/2" wide ribbon border around the perimeter, but this is not necessary although it will give a finished look to the piece.

6 - The next step is to apply 1/4" to 3/8" diameter metal spots using the design shown in this illustration or something similar. These are sewn on through the top layer or cover. Small silver brooches will substitute or may be used in combination with silver buttons. A silver, German "silver," or pewter band is fitted around the center part of the bow that is about 1/2" to 1" wide.

7 - A trailer portion may be made of one large ribbon the width of the bottom or a combination of ribbons to form one large piece. The trailer ribbons hang down the back and extend to the calf of the leg. These are attached to the underside of the hairbow by folding raw edges under and blind stitching. The trailer can be decorated with silver buttons and brooches spaced down the length of the ribbons, as shown. And the ends of the ribbons are cut into V-shapes from which tin cones are attached.

KEKENOKESHEWA

This type of ensemble was worn throughout the Great Lakes and into the western prairies from about 1790 through the removal period of the 1830s and 1840s.

HAIR - Plaited and tied in back with a hairbow

EAR BOBS - Single silver cone and ball on each ear

NECKLACES - Glass trade beads in graduated layers

BLOUSE - Caped trade shirt fashioned after the Revolutionary War hunting frock worn by men. Several layers of ruffles often form the cape draping over the shoulders and decorated with silver brooches

SKIRT - Wrap-around wool skirt decorated with silk ribbons on each side of the fabric. Worn with pattern on left or right side of the front

SASH - Finger-woven wool sash in chevron pattern tied around the waist and holding a tobacco pouch and ermine-skin fetish

LEGGINGS - Made of wool fabric of matching or contrasting color sewn into a tube with outside wing flaps decorated with diamond-cut ribbon applique

MOCCASINS - Center seam one-piece with quillwork and ribbon trimmed ears or wing flaps.

The Huron of Quebec and Lorette, the Miami and Potawatomi of Indiana and Michigan, and the Illini and Kaskaskia of the prairies as well as the Delaware, Eastern Dakota and Menominee of Wisconsin all wore variations of this ensemble during the last decade of the 18th century and the first half of the 19th. This highly decorated and embellished outfit was worn for special occasions and less decorated versions were worn for everyday work and daily life activities.

FIGURE 49

FIGURE 49

LA BLONDE RICHARDVILLE
1790-1847

Among the members of the tribes in the region of the Great Lakes were many Indians of French and Indian blood. However, although their ancestors were of French descent, it was the British and the new American government that influenced them during this period. Just prior to the final removal of the tribes from their native homes in the Great Lakes, the clothing of the tribes reached a sort of peak in style and decoration. This came about in the form of abundant use of trade silver, silk ribbon applique, trade blankets for matchcoats and capotes, trade beads of varying colors and designs, and the trend to use multiple layers of silver cones on each ear for decoration during festive occasions. This "Eastern" appearance was soon to be affected by the influence of the west, thus changing the styles and appearance of the Great Lakes Indians forever.

WILSA or *HAIR* - Tied behind the head high on the back of the neck if single, or low when married

HAIRBOW - Hourglass-shaped, wool-covered leather with silk ribbon trailer hanging down in back. This was tied to the braid with a leather thong or ribbon

EAR BOBS - Multiple use of silver ball and cone earrings on each ear

NLAPKAKANI or *SHIRT* - Caped calico trade shirts embellished with various sizes of ring brooches (*Wapikisolia*), and of up to 10" diameter cut-out brooches

KOLAMA or *MATCHCOAT* - Witney or other trade blanket used as robe or shawl over the whole ensemble

METACOSHEE or *WRAP-AROUND SKIRT* - Wool stroud cloth decorated down both edges with silk ribbonwork and also around the hem with a different pattern of ribbonwork. 1/2 inch silver ring brooches are pinned in geometric designs just above the ribbonwork all around the skirt. Tin cones dangle from the hem of the skirt for added affect in dances and ceremonies

ATASIMA or *LEGGINGS* - Tight fitted tubular leggings tied on with garters just below the knee and decorated with silk ribbonwork

MAKISSIN or *MOCCASINS* - One-piece center seam moccasins with ribbonwork on the ears or flaps. In winter, lined with rabbit skin with hair on, or layers of moss or cattail fluff

FIGURE 50

FIGURE 50

Footwear was designed to fit the location and environment of the tribe that lived there and as such, soft-soled moccasins were useful in wooded areas for walking on leaves, pine needles and soft grass.

Both Indian men and women in the Great Lakes region wore moccasins made of elk, deer, or buffalo. Several styles were very popular and seen frequently among the Hurons, Miami, Santee, Illini, Menominee and other tribes of the 18th and 19th centuries. A one-piece, center seam pucker-toe style with ear flaps was common, with some variations among each tribe.

MIAMI STYLE collected from the Iroquois (1890) at the
Chicago Field Museum of Natural History
Ribbonwork Cuffs - Center Seam (Quillwork strip covers center seam)

MIAMI MAN'S MOCCASIN, Circa 1850, Length 9 1/2"
Cranbrook Institute of Science, Bloomfield Hills, Michigan
Silk Ribbon applique on flaps. Center Seam, edge beading on flaps

FIGURE 51 & 52

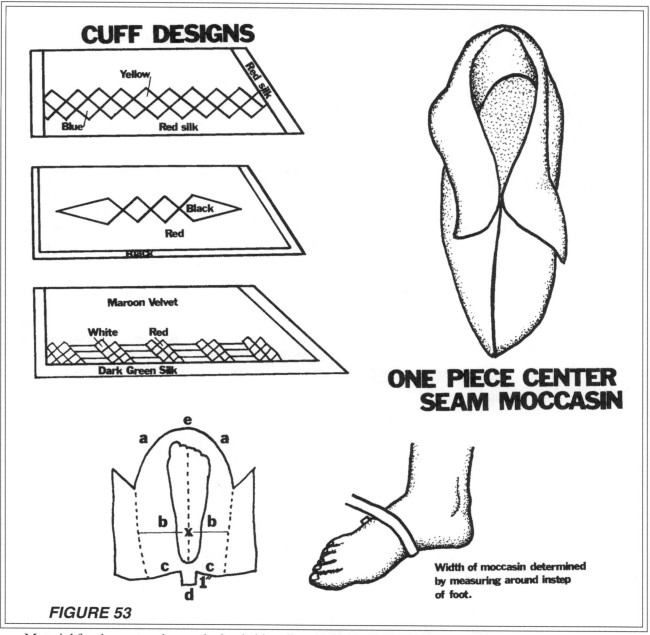

CUFF DESIGNS

Yellow

Blue

Red silk

Red silk

Black

Red

BACK

Maroon Velvet

White   Red

Dark Green Silk

ONE PIECE CENTER SEAM MOCCASIN

Width of moccasin determined by measuring around instep of foot.

FIGURE 53

Material for the moccasin may be buckskin, elk or buffalo. If the leather is commercial-tanned, use the flesh side (suede side) out as this will more closely resemble brain-tanned hide.

An old style of moccasin was made with a straight, puckered seam up the center front and a plain seam up the heel. This one-piece moccasin has a characteristic pointed toe and the right and left foot patterns are the same.

1 - Distance X between b--b should be the circumference of the instep

2 - 1" between heel tracing to heel flap

3 - 1 1/2" between toe tracing to point e

4 - Trace pattern on the leather and cut out

5 - Moccasin is folded inside out along the center line (d-e). This curved line is stitched with 1/8" stitches by joining b--b. Sew toward the toe which is pulled up with puckers.

6 - The heel seam (c--c) is stitched together with the heel flap (d) on the inside as the moccasin is sewn inside-out.

The moccasins were often decorated with quillwork and beadwork along and on either side of the toe seam. The cuff was decorated with quills, ribbon applique, beads or a combination of all of these. The cuff might also be made separately of wool or velvet.

67

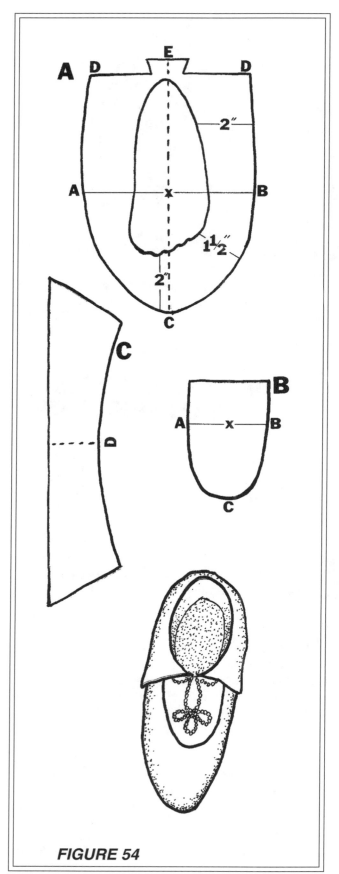

FIGURE 54

WOODLAND MOCCASIN

This is a three-piece, soft-sole, vamped (tongued) moccasin that was typical of those worn by the Wood-land Tribes of the Great Lakes Region. The materials for construction may be any soft, medium weight leather.

1 - The pattern is made with a foot tracing as shown in Figure 54

2 - Distance X on the foot pattern (A) and X on the vamp (tongue) pattern (B) should equal the total instep circumference plus a seam allowance

3 - The cuff is made from a single piece of leather (C) that is long enough to go around the ankle.

4 - To assemble the moccasin, baste sole (A) to vamp (B) at the points a-a, b-b and c-c with the flesh side out

5 - Use whip stitches about 1/8" apart to stitch the seam as you pucker the sole piece as evenly as possible. The vamp piece is not puckered.

6 - The cuff seam (C) is begun at the center of the heel (d-d) and then sewn around the top of the moccasin in both directions to points a and b where the vamp joins the sole

7 - The seams are pounded flat except for the seam joining the cuff and the upper which is left as a roll

8 - A two foot leather thong is attached under the cuff at the heel so that it can be crossed in front of the angle and tied under the rear cuff.

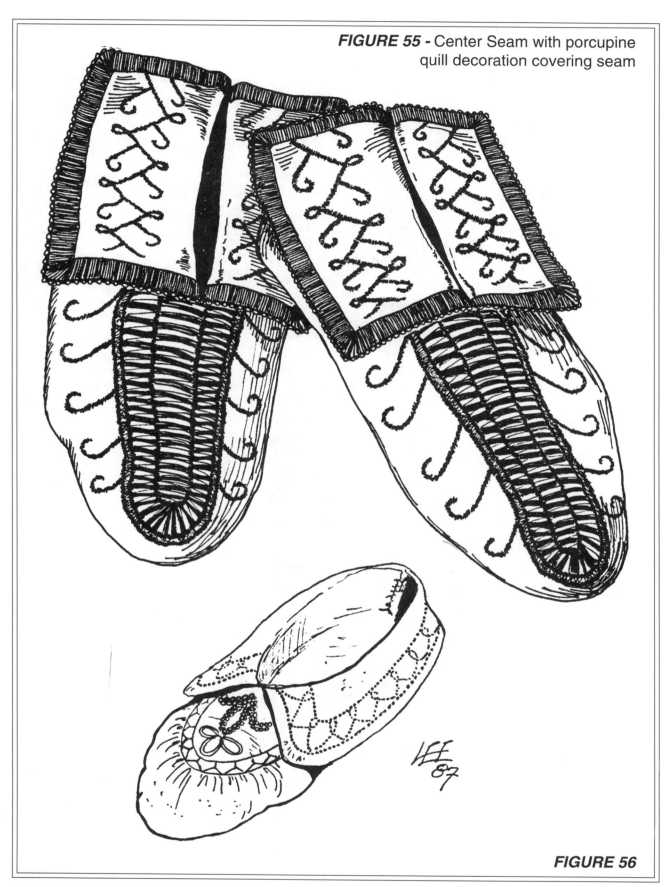

FIGURE 55 - Center Seam with porcupine quill decoration covering seam

LEE 87

FIGURE 56

69

FIGURE 57

MEN'S CLOTHING

As the French and the British fought for control of the allegiance of the various Indian tribes by offering presents to them, the Indian men still preferred their own simple mode of dress. Breechclout, leggings, moccasins and a blanket obtained from the traders was given over and over as the basic outfit of a warrior (*Jacobs* 1967: pp. 50-51).

In contrast, on ceremonial occasions the male Indian attire was greatly changed. Some of the young men wore as many as twelve gorgets around their neck and down the front of a fancy coat of fine scarlet cloth. Under this coat often was a flowery chintz or linen shirt with ruffles. Iroquois sachems prized elaborate silk waistcoats trimmed with lace and gold that were worn over the shirts.

The French were in competition with the English in giving native leaders the finest suits of clothes available. During the 1750s, the Indians desired French fabrics because they were of better quality than the British merchandise. French blankets and ratteen, which was used for stockings, were in particular demand and at times the French gave the Indian men a complete outfit, called the Aduapou, which consisted of a blanket, shirt, leggings, shoes, and a breechclout. The British took advantage of the desire for French goods by confiscating French woolens. William Johnson was able to purchase French woolens, captured by British war vessels, at almost the same price as English blankets (*Jacobs* 1967: pp. 69-70).

Edmond Atkins, superintendent of the southern fur trade in the mid-18th century, included waistcoats of scarlet, blue or green trimmed with cheap, gaudy lace, and yellow, silver or gold buttons. The shirts, some of which were ruffled, were ordered of Scotch or Irish linen. For the Indian man, who seldom wore a chapeau, gaudy hats were a special treat - especially those laced with gold and silver tinsel. Gartering and ribbons of the most striking hues were in great demand for lacing jackets and other clothing. The Indians often specified a desire for goods of particular colors and designs. It is of interest to observe that their tastes were catered to even in those cases where they demanded a special kind of stripe or print (*Jacobs* 1967: pp. 51-52).

In order to influence the Miami confederacy to the British side in 1749, the Miami sachem, Old Britain (or Le Damoiselle, as he was know to the French), distributed secret flags, belts, pipes, strings of red-painted wampum, and blankets of red and black cloth to all of the tribes under his leadership. British traders were supplying some 80 Ohio and Lake Erie villages with 40 horse loads of goods at a time. To counteract this influence by the British, the French Governor General again resorted to the use of presents giving the leaders of the Miami confederacy Le Gris, Le Pied Froid, or Le Demoiselle, "a complete chief's ensemble" (*New York Colonial Documents*, X, 139).

John Heckewelder was very interested in the clothing of the Indians that he stayed with, particularly the Delaware on the Muskingum River. He noted that the wealthy adorn themselves with blankets, plain or ruffled shirts and leggings trimmed with ribbons or gartering of various colors, beads and silver brooches. The trimming was arranged by the women, who, as well as the men, knew how to dress themselves in style. He also noted, "...their moccasins, are embroidered in the neatest manner, with coloured porcupine quills, and ... almost entirely covered with various trinkets; they have, moreover, a number of little bells and brass thimbles fixed round their ankles, which when they walk, make a tinkling noise ..." (*Wallace* 1985: pp. 52-53).

Thus, for a single night's frolic, a whole day was spent in what they called dressing, in which each participant strives to out do the others with elaborate paints, bells, trims, brightly colored shirts and leggings. When the men paint their thighs, legs and breast, they generally, after laying on a thin coat of a dark color and sometimes of a white clay, dip their fingers in black or red paint, and drawing it on the outspread fingers, bring the streaks to a serpentine form. Neither are they all alike in taste, every one dressing himself according to his fancy, or the custom of the tribe to which he belongs (*Wallace* 1985: pp. 53-54).

Among the Chippewa, men's clothing was basically the same as above. Additionally, the leggings were rather tight and did not lap far at the sides and extended from mid-thigh to the ankle and were held in place by a thong tied to the belt. A band or thong was tied below the knee.

Winter coats and pointed hoods were made from old blankets. The coats were belted and the pointed hoods were often made to extend down to the waist. A muskrat skin or deerskin was tanned with the hair on and worn as a "chest protector" by men on hunting

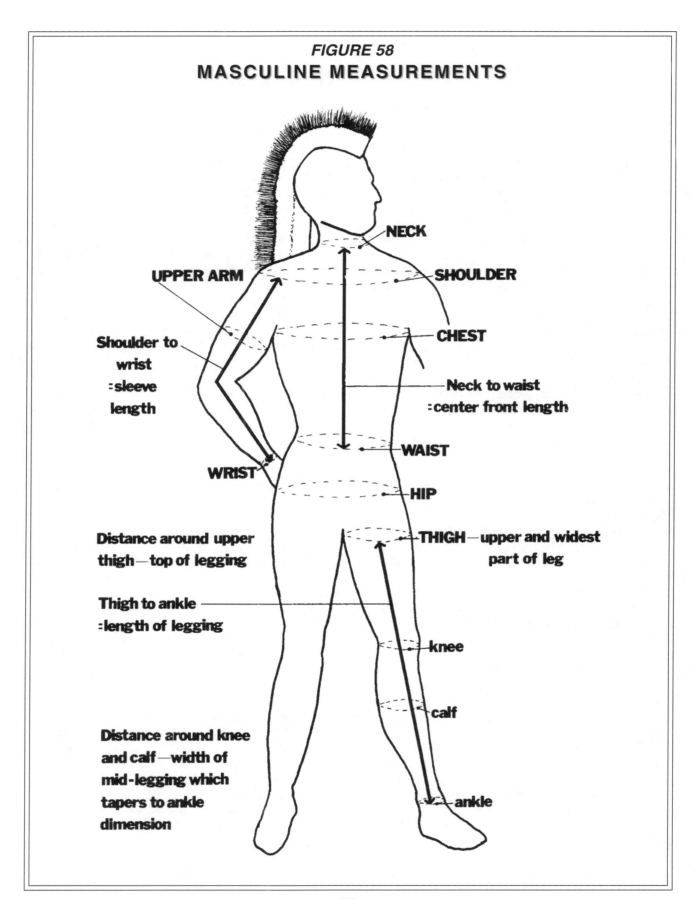

FIGURE 58
MASCULINE MEASUREMENTS

NECK

UPPER ARM

SHOULDER

Shoulder to
wrist
=sleeve
length

CHEST

Neck to waist
=center front length

WRIST

WAIST

HIP

Distance around upper
thigh—top of legging

THIGH—upper and widest
part of leg

Thigh to ankle
=length of legging

knee

calf

Distance around knee
and calf—width of
mid-legging which
tapers to ankle
dimension

ankle

72

expeditions and was occasionally worn by women. Rabbit skins with the hair on were placed inside the moccasins to make them warmer in winter (*Densmore* 1979: p. 31).

Further descriptions of men's clothing came from George Winter when he visited the Miami villages on the Wabash in the 1830s. Jean Baptiste Brouillette, who was of French and Indian descent, was described by Winter in this manner: "His tout ensemble was unique as his aboriginal costume was expensive and showy. He wore round his head a rich figured crimson shawl a' la turban, with long and flowing ends gracefully falling over the shoulders; silver ornaments or clusters of ear bobs, testified their weight by a partial elongation of the ears. He wore a fine frock coat of the latest fashion ... His *pesmokin* or shirt was white, spotted with small red figures overhanging very handsome blue leggings, "winged" with very rich silk ribbons of prismatic hues, exhibiting the squaw's skillful needle work. A handsome red silk sash was thrown gracefully over his left shoulder, and passing over his breast and under the right arm, with clusters of knots, and fringed masses, gave point a style to Brouillette's tall and majestic figure" (*Lafayette Courier*, July 1867).

As a final tribute to the Indians of the Great Lakes, just prior to their forced removal from there, one more description of men's clothing comes from Thomas Roche who participated in an adoption ceremony among the Miami in the early 1840s. "The young Indian fops would appear in their best, which was usually a fine frock coat with vest to match; leggings, upon which some artistic woman had spend many an hour to ornament in diamonds, stripes and blocks (all ribbonwork), the edges trimmed with beads. This ornamental work was always upon the flap or seam. Whole width of three-fourths cassimer was used for each legging, which were made to fit as tight as a dude's trowsers, which would leave quite a field for ornamental work.

"The shirt was also quite a prominent part of the dress of fancy young Indians. This must always be calico of fine quality, usually a light color with small set figures, made with ruffled front; it was long enough to come to the knees. All below the vest was in plain view if the coat was unbuttoned. For footwear, moccasins were the proper thing, trimmed to match the leggings. When he had each cheek striped with vermillion, like bars in a jail window, and small dots in each square, a stripe down the center of his nose, a tinge around the eyes, a good supply of rings in his ears and one in his nose, he was in a presentable condition and ready to be seen." (*Brandt and Fuller* 1887: p. 318)

MEN'S CLOTHING AND ADORNMENT

HAIRSTYLES

18th century illustrations show that eastern Indian men wore a hairstyle requiring the pulling or plucking out of most of the hair except for a scalplock which was about 4" square or round on the crown of the head. According to the Journal of James Smith, or Scoouwa, who was a captive of the Delaware Indians in 1755: "... a number of Indians collected about me, and one of them began to pull the hair out of my head. He had some ashes on a piece of bark, in which he frequently dipped his fingers in order to take the firmer hold ... as if he were plucking a turkey, until he had all the hair clean out of my head, except a small spot about three or four inches square on my crown; this they cut off with a pair of scissors, excepting three locks, which they dressed up in their own mode. Two of these they wrapped round with a narrow beaded garter made by themselves for that purpose, and the other they plaited at full length, and then stuck it full of silver brooches..." (*Drimmer* 1961: p. 31).

Some eastern warriors chose to wear two long braids, but before battle they selected a large tuft on the top of their head and braided half of it. They then wound it with bark to make it stand up. Often, the top braid was then decorated with feathers, brooches, ribbons, beads or quills (*Bender* 1980: pp. 15-17).

EAR MUTILATION

The ears were sometimes cut at the time of birth or shortly thereafter during a special ceremony and a roll of birchbark placed into the perforation to both absorb the blood and hold the slit open until it could heal and ornamental beads could replace the bark (*Echert* 1971: p. 13).

Distended earlobes or the cutting of the warrior's earlobes was practiced eagerly and was much more common before the time of the French and Indian War. John Heckewelder noted that the reasons for laying this custom aside were that the operation was painful, not only when performed, but until the ears were perfectly healed. Even more importantly, the warriors often lost that part of their ear which was separated from the solid part, when it was torn off by the bushes or fell off due to frostbite.

HEAD COVERINGS

One popular head ornament was the ***porcupine-***

OKIMA - CHIEF
18th CENTURY

Often treaty negotiations required the presence of tribal leaders who were gifted with silver brooches, pipe tomahawks, linen trade shirts, waistcoats, and wool fabric among the many items given for their part in getting members of the tribe to sign the agreement

HEADGEAR - Round or oval porcupine hair roach was often used as a symbol of leadership or past accomplishments as a warrior and then surrounded by a finger-woven sash wrapped turban fashion on the outside of the head

EAR BOBS - Four seperate ball and cone ear bobs are worn dangling from each ear

TRADE SHIRT - Silk or linen trade shirt with ruffled front and cuffs give the wearer a certain status

WAISTCOAT - Or vest, was an item of the fur trade from as early as the French and Indian War Period. Decorated with silver brooches

FINGER-WOVEN SASH - A second finger-woven sash was often worn around the waist tied beneath the waistcoat

BREECHCLOUT - Wool fabric decorated with silk ribbons worn between the legs and held at the waist with a thong

LEGGINGS - Center seam leggings of wool fabric sewn into tubes that have contrasting color trim on both sides of seam and edge beaded on both sides as well

GARTERS - Finger-woven garters tied just below the knee

MOCCASINS - The center seam moccasins have flaps or ears hidden beneath the leggings that rest over the top of the moccasins

FIGURE 59

74

FIGURE 59

EASTERN WOODLAND WARRIOR
1745-1795

It was not uncommon to see woodland warriors dressed in nothing more than a breechclout and moccasins. However, often particular styles of headgear, paint and other adornment was selected by the men to help them gather strength and spiritual guidance in life-threatening situations.

HAIR - All but a scalplock on the crown of the head has been shaved or plucked out

ROACH - Porcupine guard hair and deer hair roach tied to the scalplock produces a striking headpiece for certain warriors in the east

FACE - Permanent tattoos and repeated face paintings such as lines and dark colorations around the eyes often give a warrior a fierce and frightening appearance to the enemy in battle

DISTENDED EAR LOBES - When Indian children are born, the boys are taken by an adult and their ears slit and a piece of rolled up bark was stuck in the slit to hold it out and absorb the blood. When removed, the warrior often wrapped the distended lobe with quills, ear wires, silver rings, and ear wheels

BODY PAINT - Often warriors were permanently tattooed with a burning ember and charcoal symbols of their clan, spiritual guides and other emblems from their daily life to ward off evil spirits and weaknesses that often occur in man

MATCHCOAT - Stroud cloth or blankets were often wrapped around the body for additional warmth and fastened with a brooch just under the chin

BREECHCLOUT - A 12"-14" wide strip of wool cloth about 50" long that passes between the legs and is held in place at the waist with a leather thong or sash. The edges are usually decorated with wool braid or silk ribbon trim

LEGGINGS - Wool trade cloth leggings were worn tight fitting to the leg up over the knee several inches with wing flap on the outside, slightly decorated with wool braid. The garters are finger-woven with beads interwoven throughout with otter or mink flap hanging down the center front

LOWER BODY PAINT or *TATTOOING* - Lines, animals or plant figures often used as part of a warriors' strength in battle or on the hunt

MOCCASINS - Center seam, one piece woodland style with wing flaps decorated with beads. Center insert decorated with quills

TRADE RIFLE - Given in trade or as gifts to various warriors was often used in battle against those who gave the weapons

FINGER-WOVEN STRAP - Worn bandolier style over one shoulder and holds powder horn and hunting pouch

KNIFE SHEATH - Decorated with quills and edge beads and hangs from the sash or thong around the waist

FIGURE 60

FIGURE 60

WOODLAND WARRIOR 1745-1795

Ready for battle, many warriors were armed in their own unique fashion. From the Seneca, Cayhuga, Delaware, Miami and Shawnee, to the Ojibwa, Ottawa, Menominee and Potawatomi of the northern lakes, the warriors gained strength and spiritual enlightenment from their adornment. They also used the garrish embellishments to show the spirits that they honored them as they risked their lives on *Mother Earth* for what each believed in.

HAIR - Long hair was not the fashion. Clipped or plucked hair often left the warrior with strands of hair standing on the crown of his head, with other strands long and braided dangling free. Still other hair locks were wrapped with quills forcing them to stand up

EAR BOBS - Silver cones were worn on each ear

FACE PAINT - Staggering black or vermillion lines were often added to the whole effect of a warrior's preparation for battle

NECKLACE - Medicine bag fastened around the neck contained herbs and charms to aid in the warrior's quest; past accomplishments in the hunt are shown off when a warrior dons a bear claw or badger claw necklace; often warriors are given peace medals when signing treaties and show them off when engaging the enemy in battle

ARM BANDS - Bands of highly polished and engraved silver often adorn upper arms of the warriors

EDGE BEAD SASH - Often attached to hunting bags, quivers and powder horns

FINGER-WOVEN SASH - Worn around the waist and tied on one side

HUNTING BAG - Wool or skin bag decorated with braid, edge beads and quills

BREECHCLOUT - Primarily a masculine garment, this consists of a 12" wide piece of cloth up to 54" long passing between the legs and held in place at the waist with a leather thong

LEGGINGS - Warriors and some *courier du bois*, traders and militia dressed in "Indian-style" and often wore skin leggings for battle and hunting up until the beginning of the 19th century. These were held in place with finger-woven garters just under the knee

MOCCASINS - Rather plain single piece, center seam moccasins with simple braid around the flap edge were more practical for battle

FIGURE 61

FIGURE 61

OKIMA 1790-1845
KASKASKIA - PEORIA - MIAMI - POTAWATOMI - ILLINI

Village leaders (*Okima*) received influence from ceremonial deference, but had little effective power. The person occupying this position was a man of proper character who was a senior member of the clan that owned the office, yet the occupant was selected from several possible candidates by the village; he did not acquire the office by birthright.

Okima were obligated to repeat to his council of warriors all questions he was asked and his responses and there were things he could not speak about without first securing their permission. Powers of the chief depended on his personal influence because he held no formal authority. A large part of the leader's influence rested on the degree of supernatural power he controlled, that is, his own "*manito*" or spirit power as measured by his successes.

The chief was aided in government tasks by a council of adult males who expressed public opinion and validated decisions. There was also a specialized council composed of the more successful warriors with their own songs and dances, who exercised police functions.

ALANYA - MIAMI MAN
OKIMA - CHIEF
WIWISAKWADSIONI - TURBAN FROM SILK SCARF
WAPIKISOLIA - SILVER RING
NAPINAKANI - SHIRT
PIITENIKOC - COAT
PWAHKAHNAH - PIPE
APWAKANIMOTAI - LEATHER POUCH
AKOTAM - BREECHCLOUT
ATASIMA - LEGGINGS
NIPITAWISEOETO - RIBBONWORK
MAKISSINI - MOCCASIN

FIGURE 62

FIGURE 62

HEAD COVERINGS

There were a variety of head pieces and forms of embellishment used by the tribes around the Great Lakes in the 18th and 19th centuries.

1 - *PORCUPINE GUARD HAIR ROACH* - Porcupine guard hair and deer hair sewn to a braided base is attached to a scalplock with a bone pin and held there with a roach spreader of a scapula bone or trade silver. This is surrounded by a finger-woven sash made of several colors of bright wool, wrapped in folds around the wearer's head. Strands of wampum are attached to the top of the ears just below the turban.

2 - *SILK TURBAN* - Plain or print silk is wrapped over the head in layers and tied in one of several ways. In this case, the loose ends are tied in front over the forehead. Ostrich plumes are tucked into the folds of the turban and drape down or stand up over the back of the head.

3 - *TURBAN* - Silk fabric is sometimes draped over the front of the wearer's head resting just above his eyebrows and the ends resting over the back of the neck and shoulders. Over this sits a fur turban of otter or beaver. A highly polished engraved silver crown sits over the top of the whole ensemble. Silver cones dangle from the crown over the silk scarf.

FIGURE 63

82

FIGURE 64

83

HEAD COVERINGS

1 - *SILK TURBAN* - A common form of head wrap consists of a silk scarf or shawl wrapped around the head several times and tied in such a way that the ends of the silk fabric flow either down the side of the head or down the back.

2 - *OTTER TURBAN* - Otter fur is another common head covering worn by warriors prior to battle or after. The tail is decorated with white edge beads or quills. A round porcupine guard hair roach is tied to a hair lock and held in place with a cloth-covered leather band decorated with quillwork and brooches. Ostrich plumes and an eagle feather are tucked into the base of the roach.

3 - *ROACH AND OTTER TURBAN OVER SILK SCARF* - Silk is tied over the head first, then an otter turban open in the center is worn around that. Additionally, a silver band or crown surround the hair roach. Silver cone dangles are attached to the ears just below the turban.

4 - *DECORATED SCALPLOCK* - All hair is plucked or shaved from the head except about a four inch square on the crown. This is left to grow and then is braided. Often the scalplock is decorated with silver ring brooches of varying sizes. Eagle feathers are tucked into the top of the braided hair. Distended or cut ear lobes are also common among the men. The ear lobes are pierced and silver crosses or cone ear bobs are worn from each ear.

FIGURE 65

FIGURE 65

HEAD COVERINGS

A - *WRAPPED SILK TURBAN* - Use silk fabric or shawl 50" to 60" long and about 20" wide minimum. Start by placing the center of the fabric over the top of the head and hold it there while bringing both ends to the back of the head. Cross them and bring them forward, pulling tightly at the same time. After bringing ends forward, cross them once again, and bring them to the back of the head again and tie or secure in the folds of the fabric. The ends fall freely over the back of the neck and shoulders.

B - *SILK SCARF* - Use silk fabric or shawl 30" square minimum and fold in half diagonally forming a triangle. Place the center of the folded edge over the top of the head with the edge at a comfortable distance just above the eyebrows. Then, bring the ends of the triangle to the back of the head and tie in a knot tucking the point of the scarf into the knot. Allow the ends to flow freely down the back. Tuck ostrich plumes into the knot and pin silver brooches to the top and front of the scarf.

FIGURE 66

FIGURE 66

hair roach. It was made from guard hair from the porcupine, deer hair, or horse hair tied to a cord, like a long fringe. This cord was then coiled and sewn so that it could be formed to be slightly concave on the underside to conform to the wearer's head. It could also be manipulated to become convex and stored on a kind of wrapped wooden club. The roach base had a small hole in the front whereby the scalplock was pushed through it and held in place with a piece of bone and this secured the roach in place. To keep the roach spread, a roach spreader was used which was made of bone, antler or trade silver. This was also fastened on with the scalplock.

Mounted on the spreader inside the outer fringes of the roach was a socket made of a turkey leg bone, and in this a single eagle tail feather was set so as to revolve with the wearer's movement. Only one feather was worn with this headdress in this region. This plume distinguished the warrior and was only laid on when he was going out to war, as this transferred the courage of the eagle to him.

Sometimes, when available, the Indian would substitute the hairs from the beard of the wild tom turkey for the guard hairs of the porcupine. This would signal to the other men in his band that he was an accomplished hunter since the turkey was a very wary bird while the porcupine could be killed with a stick. The *turkey-beard roach* was a status symbol and made in the same manner as the porcupine hair roach.

An *otterskin cap* was sometimes worn turban style around the crown of the head. This was sometimes worn in conjunction with a silk scarf decorated with silver brooches. The otter fur turban was sometimes decorated with edge beads, silver crown or band around the outside and set over the silk scarf to form an outer rim. Ostrich plumes often were tucked into the folds of the fur or silk in front or in back of the head.

The *gastoweh*, a headdress so named by the Iroquois, was also adapted by the Shawnee, Miami, Ottawa and other eastern Great Lakes Tribes. It is built on a framework or base of ash splints, like those used in baskets. One splint circles the wearer's head and two more cross over it, one from front to back, the other from side to side. At the point where the two cross on top, a number of stripped hawk feathers are attached in a radial pattern. Also attached at the top so as to slant backwards in a bone socket, is a single eagle tail feather fixed in it so as to revolve with the wearer's movement.

The wooden framework was covered with trade cloth or silk, and is circled at the bottom by a silver band with fancy cut-out work.

Finger-woven sashes were often wrapped around the wearer to serve as a decorative headdress with ostrich plumes tucked into the folds of a *turban*. Often silver brooches were pinned on the sash as well. Again, this was sometimes worn alone or wrapped around a silk scarf (turban) or a fur turban or hair roach.

Silk scarfs or shawls were often folded and wrapped in several ways around a man's head and embellished with silver brooches pinned at random. Sometimes a silver band or crown was worn around the outside of the silk turban. Ostrich plumes were often tucked into the folds of the silk protruding out the back or tucked in the front folds so that the plumes fall slightly back over the top of the crown. The remaining lengths of cloth were simply left to hang or trail down the neck and shoulders of the wearer.

Cylinders made from birch bark covered with trade cloth and decorated with quills, beads and feathers were worn as a *headdress* by some of the warriors in the Great Lakes region. One example of this is an Ojibwa headdress covered with blue blanket-cloth, appliques of red and green wool tape, wool and cotton cloth, silk ribbon, and white glass beads. The upper mandibles and crowns of four woodpeckers are attached at the front, with yellow and blue silk ribbons threaded through the nostrils. Hawk, eagle and eagle-down feathers and several animal tails were attached around the top of the head piece; quill-wrapped wooden splints are attached to the eagle feathers (*Brasser* 1976: p. 95).

A *leather headdress* or skin cap fitted to the wearer's head was also worn that was heavily adorned with quills, feathers, and ribbons. The cap was made from tanned skins, tapered to a fringed point at the back and seamed down the center of the crown. A broad band of tanned skin was attached around the rim, decorated with quill-wrapped strips of rawhide. Truncated, triangular-shaped skin tabs of smoked skin and red-dyed feathers were inserted between the band and cap. Feathers were stitched to the base of vegetable-fiber thread. Large peacock feathers were originally also secured here. Tassels of metal cones, quill-wrapped thongs, and hair were attached to the cap front. It was secured to the head with a leather thong (*Brasser* 1976: p. 114).

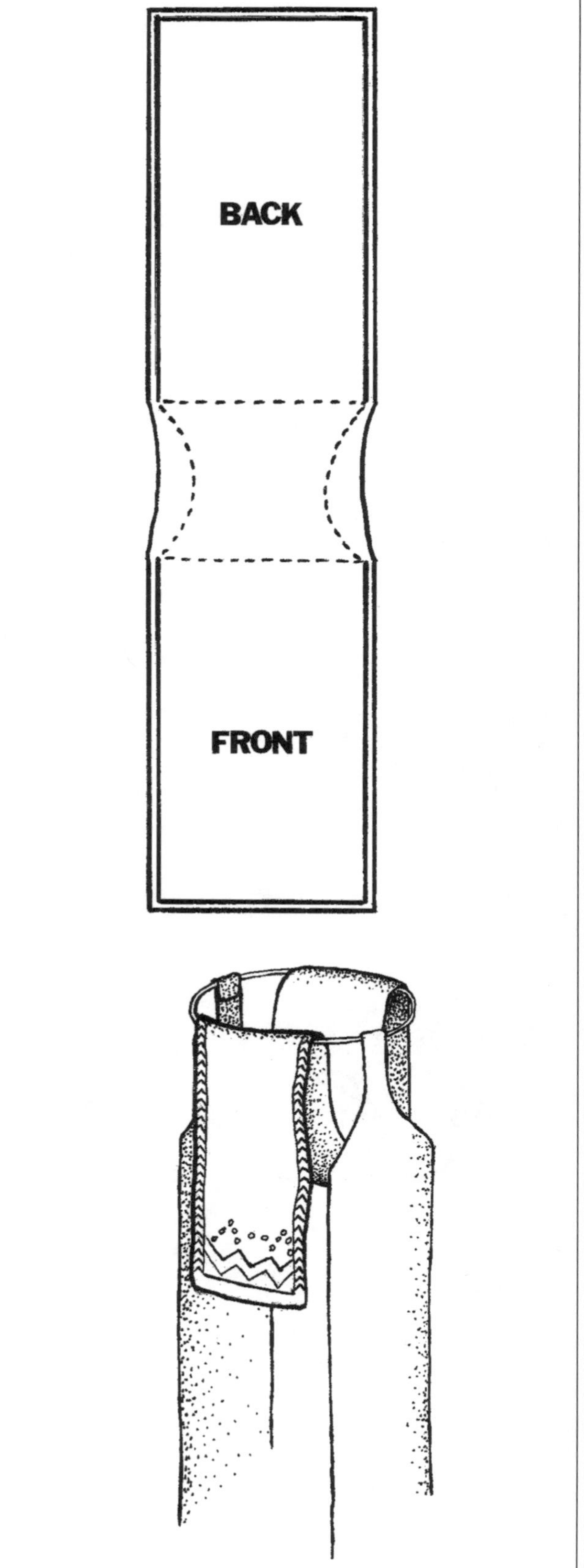

BACK

FRONT

FIGURE 67

BREECHCLOUT

The basic male garment of the Indian men of the Great Lakes Region was the breechclout. Originally, the breechclout consisted of a narrow skin fitted between a man's legs and held at the waist with a leather thong. This created a front flap and a back flap which provided some additional covering.

The breechclout worn in the 18th century and early 19th century did not change form or function, just the material from which it was made. Trade cloth was introduced and wool virtually replaced the skin clout of previous generations. It was often decorated in a variety of ways. Wool braid, silk ribbon, silver brooches and beads were used to embellish this garment.

Although the breechclout has been used by Indian men from many tribes all over the region, it seems to have been the only waist-fitting garment worn by the men of the Great Lakes tribes during this time period. Among some Algonquin speaking people, the string that the breechclout was tied on was as important as the clout itself. Some of the older customs imply that if they took off the string, the men would lose their manhood.

Early 18th century paintings reveal that the breechclout was quite small, perhaps being only 6" to 8" in width and 8" or 9" in length. This was probably due to the fact that the men were using a single width of fabric for the entire length of the breechclout.

While a good description and/or example has not yet been found, at least two sources indicate that in some cases in the Great Lake Region women wore a breechclout of some sort. Of these, Samuel de Champlain writes of Ottawa women in 1615, "... women wore a leather breechclout reaching to the middle of their thighs ..."

In order to construct a breechclout, you must first calculate the length needed: Measure from the bottom of the feet to the top of the head. This will make a breechclout that reaches approximately to mid-thigh length. The width is usually dependent upon the wearer, but the average is 12" - 14" wide; the crotch may be tapered and lined with cotton for comfort (see *Figure 67*). The breechclout is held in place just below the waist, at the pelvic bone, with a leather thong or wool braid. Leggings tie to the same leather thong or sash on the outside of each thigh. The thong fits under the front flap, runs around the body, under the rear flap and is tied on one side.

An alternate method of securing the breechclout is to permanently attach leather thongs or wool ties to each side of the front flap and to each side of the back flap.

The breechclout was often decorated with edge beading, border bead applique and/or ribbonwork borders, and silver brooches similar to the embellishment

89

FIGURE 68

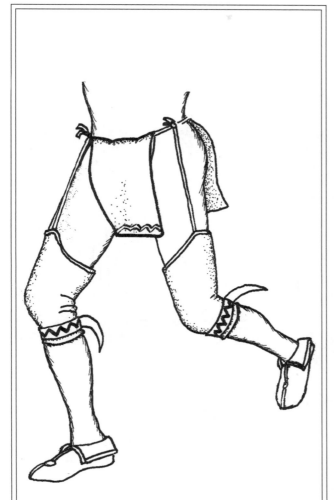

Military Issue Cotton Stockings

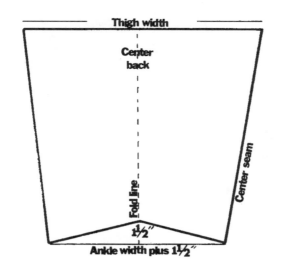

Center Seam Leggings
FIGURE 69

of women's wrap-around skirts.

MEN'S LEGGINGS

Most eastern Indians wore leggings with a breechclout. Many white men on the frontier adopted the breechclout and leggings, both for comfort and to "fit in" with the Indians, often wearing them over breeches. Generally, the leggings of the 18th century were worn just a few inches over the knee due to the fact that each legging was made of one-half of the width of a blanket issued to the Indians.

After 1800, leggings were longer due to the fact that better and bigger blankets were requested by the Indians. The top of the leggings reached higher up on the thighs, nearly reaching the hem of the breechclout.

Styles of Men's Leggings

There were two basic variations of leggings:

1 - The **Center Seam** legging is a basic, snug-fitting tube, ending in an open flap which tucks into the moccasin or sits just over the top of the moccasin. The tube is sewn in the center front, often with wool braid serving as the decorative outline on the sewn edge. A strap is attached to the outer side of each legging to be tied to the waist thong that holds the breechclout. Jonathan Carver's 1760 drawing of a Fox Indian shows this style as well as the 1820s painting by Charles Bird King. White beads, or buttons of brass, pewter, or silver were often used on both sides of the seam for decoration (*Viola* 1980: Front).

To make this style of legging, use 1 1/4 yards of wool material cut into two pieces (one for each legging). These are sewn to form a close fit to each leg just as wide as the calf. The outside flaps are sometimes added and then decorated. Be sure to sew these wrong side out with about a 1/2" seam. Turn them right side out and decorate.

2 - Variations of **Side Seam** leggings with wing flaps or tabs were used throughout the Great Lakes. Some side seam leggings were fitted to the leg tightly. On the outside was a double wing or tab that hung somewhat freely from each legging proper and some wings were composed of a flap from the back and the front stitched on the inside forming the outer seam of the leggings, but left open on the outside. Each flap was decorated independently of the other with edge beads, ribbons, brooches and braid.

Some wings were tapered out starting at the top of the outside of the leggings and ending just above the

91

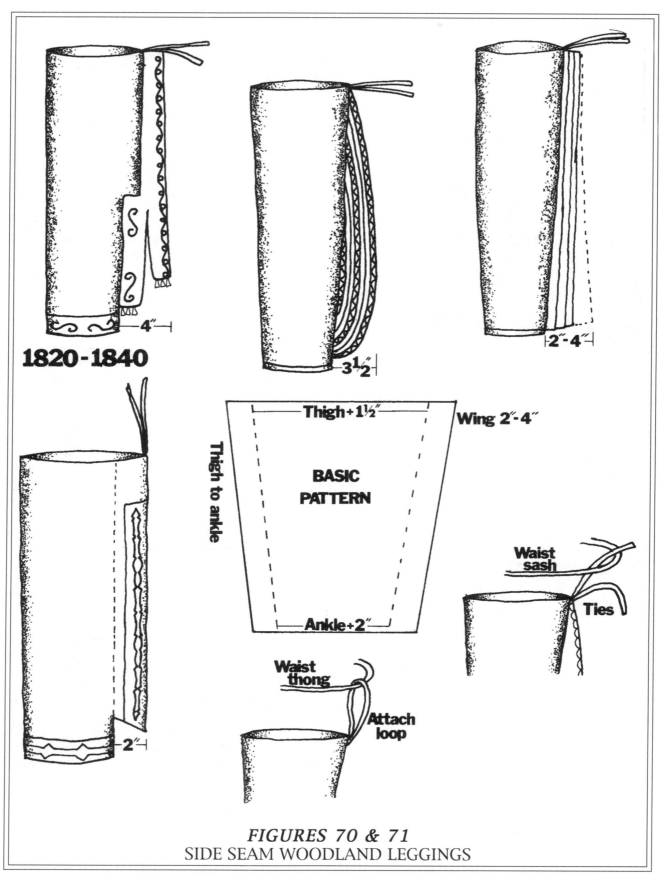

1820-1840

Thigh+1½″

Wing 2″-4″

Thigh to ankle

BASIC
PATTERN

Ankle+2″

4″

3½

2″-4″

2″

Waist
sash

Ties

Waist
thong

Attach
loop

FIGURES 70 & 71
SIDE SEAM WOODLAND LEGGINGS

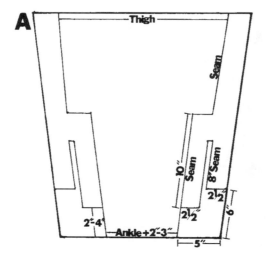

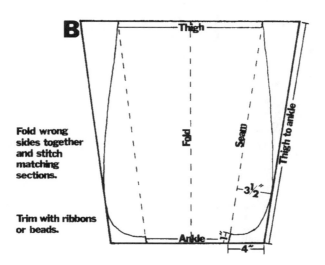

Fold wrong sides together and stitch matching sections.

Trim with ribbons or beads.

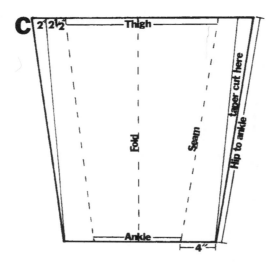

FIGURE 72

ankle where the wing curved in toward the leg. Again, ribbons, beads, and brooches were used in liberal decoration.

Still another variation was a tapered flap that was straight across the bottom, rather than curved. Garters of finger-woven designs were often tied just under the knee of each leg. Otter-tail garters were also used, decorated with edge beads and quills.

FABRICS

Deerskin or elk skin was used especially in winter. They were used in hunting or in battle where wool would be less effective. Some of these were decorated with quillwork and had very short side-seam fringe. Some of the center seam style with a front tab were decorated with quills or braid. When made of cloth, materials used included wool stroud, duffle or other blanket material.

MILITARY STOCKINGS

Military stockings made of cotton were issued to Indians during the 18th century. Colors included red, white, blue and black as well as aurora and those dyed to meet the Indians' requests. According to William Johnson in 1755, "... an Iroquois warrior was given a fine shirt, a pair of hose and ribbons, total ensemble valued at only one pound, ten shillings." Women also highly valued these military stockings.

FIGURE 72
SIDE SEAM
WOODLAND LEGGINGS
- PATTERN VARIATIONS

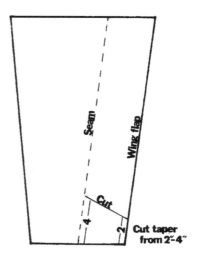

FIGURE 73

Private gifts of clothing and trade cloth were often gifted to tribal leaders by the superintendents of the fur trade. Bright calico shirts were among some of the presents given to the Indians as early as the mid-18th century and these shirts added a bit of warmth and color to the wardrobe of the fur trade era Indians of the Great Lakes.

Further, many Indians saw the benefits in imitating the dress and fashion of the government officials and traders and thus fancy shirts, waistcoats and coats were high priority items in the fur trade. When ready-made shirts were not available, fabric was requested by tribes to make shirts based on those worn by those mentioned above.

Trade shirts were made in the same style that shirts were made for settlers and soldiers with some exceptions. The shirts for the Indians were often made of "cheaper" quality fabric and gawdy prints. By 1756, Sir William Johnson had ordered some 400 shirts for gifts to be handed out to Indians in his charge and thus quantity, not quality was in demand. By the end of the French and Indian War, storehouses were literally 18th century warehouses for Indian gifts and trade items, including shirts and other woolen and linen textiles.

Some of the most requested fabrics included cotton calico and chintz in large, bright prints in reds, yellows, and blues. Plain white and beige and other solid colors often provided the perfect background for multitudes of silver brooches, gorgets and glass trade beads. Linen and muslin also were utilized and although some were plain in color, others were bright block prints typical of mid-18th century style.

Many shirts were complete with front and cuff ruffles and buttoned with antler, bone, pewter, silver or brass buttons at the wrist. Others were tied at the neck and wrists with matching fabrics or fastened just at the wrists with cuff links made from two buttons connected with a wire loop.

In making an 18th century shirt, it is suggested that you use approximately 3 1/2 yards of linen, muslin, cotton chintz or silk. Bright colors were typical of Indian use; large block print calicoes and plain white

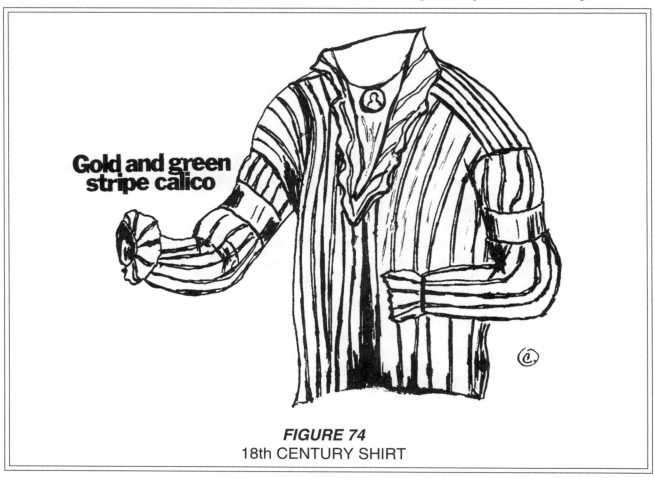

Gold and green stripe calico

FIGURE 74
18th CENTURY SHIRT

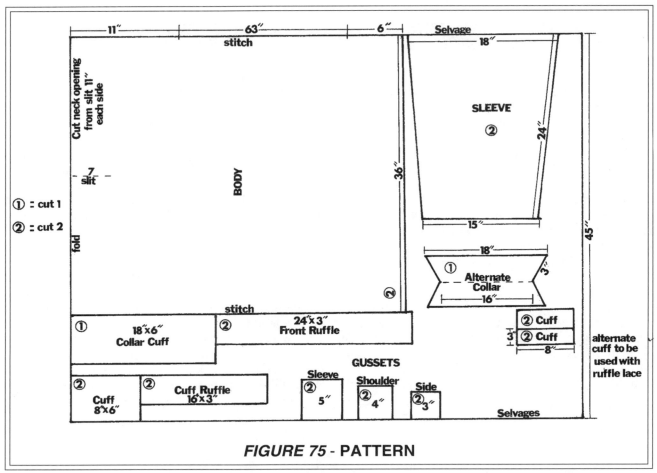

FIGURE 75 - **PATTERN**

was also used. To construct an 18th century shirt, follow the instructions given below:

1 - Cut paper pattern according to the measurements in *Figure 75* and pin together making adjustments for personal fit.

2 - Cut 7" slash center front and then 1" neck opening on each side of the slash.

3 - If front ruffle is to be added, start by folding in half, lengthwise, each ruffle with right sides together. Stitch the ends and turn the right sides out. Gather seam allowance to fit the neck slit. Pin right side of neck slit with right side of ruffle. Then stitch the seam allowance and press to inside. Repeat with the other side. If no ruffle is used, press under the 1/4" hem on each side of slit and then stitch.

4 - Prepare the shoulder gussets by folding the wrong sides together diagonally and stitch along the seam line. Insert into neckline opening and point away from neck. Stitch along seam line with right sides together.

5 - Gather the neckline to about 15" or to fit the wearer. Prepare collar or alternate tapered collar by folding in half, lengthwise, and stitch the ends with the right sides together. Turn right side out and pin into the

neck opening while adjusting the gathers evenly around the neck opening. Stitch.

6 - With the right sides of the shirt body together, stitch the side seams to within 11" of the shoulder and to within 6" of the hem. Prepare the side gusset as done with the shoulder gusset and stitch with the right sides together into the bottom of the side seams - pointed up.

7 - Prepare underarm gussets in the same manner. Fold the sleeve right sides together, lengthwise, and pin. Insert gusset at should end and stitch. Sew the sleeve seam from 6-8" above the wrist to the point of gusset for each sleeve. Note: The 6-8" opening depends on the individual as some sleeves were open almost to the gussets while others, only a few inches.

8 - Stitch a narrow, 1/4" hem on both edges from the wrist end to the start of the seam.

9 - Stitch gusset to the sleeve starting at the shoulder underarm and following around the V-shape of the joint gusset and the sleeve. Repeat this with the other sleeve. Now turn inside out.

10 - Prepare the cuffs with attached ruffles as follows: Pin the cuff sections lengthwise with right sides together and stitch the ends - allow for overlap to the bottom. Press under the seam allowance on both of the sides. Prepare the ruffle by turning the right sides

96

FIGURE 76 & 77
18th Century Men's Shirt

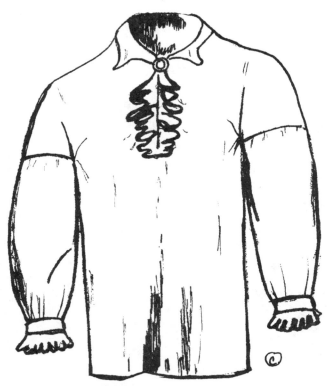

Shirt length to mid-thigh

Sleeves - full & blousy before 1800

Tied at waist with sash

Length to just above knee after 1800

together lengthwise and stitching the ends. Turn right side out. Gather at the seam allowance and fit into the cuff opening. Now blind stitch the ruffle to the cuff and then repeat for the other cuff.

11 - Attach cuff ruffles to the wrist end of the sleeve by inserting the sleeve, after gathering wrist, into the cuff. Pin this, blind stitch and then repeat with the other sleeve.

12 - A variation of the ruffle, instead of making it from the same fabric, is to replace the material with bobbin lace, 2-3" wide.

13 - A variation in sleeve fullness can be obtained by making the sleeve width up to 25" wide instead of the suggested 18" width yet still tapering to 15" at the wrist.

14 - To fit the sleeve into the shirt body, mark the center top of the sleeve and mark the center of the sleeve opening at the top. Then gather the sleeve, not the gusset, to fit the sleeve opening. Pin the sleeve to the opening with the right sides together, adjusting the gathers evenly as this is done. Then stitch the matching marks, turn inside out and repeat the above for the other sleeve.

15 - Make a narrow hem on the sides below the gussets and hem the bottom or cover the raw edges with narrow ribbons.

16 - To make a fuller and more formal shirt, some shirts were pleated at the shoulder with as many as 30 tiny pleats per inch. Also, instead of the same fabric ruffle around the front neck slit, replace with bobbin lace. Note: Indians would make special requests of shirts made in this way.

17 - The collar button, made of silver, brooch, pewter, brass, bone, antler or wood, and the loop were set at the seam where the collar joins the shirt body. Buttons made into cufflinks were often used at wrists or a button hole was made on one side of the cuff and one of the types of buttons listed above were sewn to the other side of the cuff. Other types of cuffs simply required permanently attached ties to be sewn on either side of the cuff and then it was tied together.

EIGHTEENTH CENTURY TRADE COAT

During an excavation by Michigan State University in 1968 at the Fletcher site in Bay City, Michigan, fragments of a woolen trade coat were uncovered. The Fletcher site was an historical Indian burial ground dating between 1740 and 1780. The remains of the coat, as it had been placed right side out over the body, were found with the extended burial of an adult male. The coat had been profusely decorated with "gold" lace and, due to the action of copper salts, large portions of the cloth were preserved only to the extent that they were

FIGURE 78

not entirely decomposed. The fabric was the "consistency and strength of a wet paper handkerchief."

Figure 82 is the result of restoring the coat. With the aid of the measurements of the fragments and drawings of coats of that general time period, an initial paper pattern was constructed from which a light-weight cloth model was cut and sewn together for fit and construction. Unbleached linen was cut and sewn to the design and the fragments, encased in silk, were stitched to the linen model in their correct position. By alternating between the paper patterns, the cloth model and the original, it was possible to restore an accurate pattern of the coat.

The coat is about 40 inches long. The center edge has lace from close to the shoulder bone down the front opening and on the curve of the shirt. The lace does not continue around the hem of the garment. There are five horizontal points on each side of the front and each has a single button. The pocket flaps are opposite the fifth point. The center back seam has lace from the neck down the curving tails and just below the waist are four horizontal points, two on each side.

The coat fabric is woolen, a 2/2 twill, heavily fulled. It is referred to as an 18th century fabric known as "*halfthick*." The coat is lined, at least in part, and the lining was also a 2/2 twill of lighter weight, probably "*quarter thick*." At the front edge of the coat, the lining is cut and turned under to form a hem 2 cm. deep; the lining is stitched on with a running stitch of approximately 1mm length. On the front, between the lining and the coat body, is a thin, open-weaved fabric; probably a linen starched to provide stiffening for these areas. The facing begins 1 cm. in from the front edge of the coat and extends at least 12 cm. in toward the side seam. The facing has a cut edge along the front.

The lace has a plain linen wrap and filling of thread wrapped with fine brass wire. There were two widths of lace, 2.5 cm and 4 cm. wide. The lace on the borders and seams is 2.5 cm. in width; the points and center strips on the pockets are made of the 4 cm. wide lace. The buttons are made of brass wound thread woven over a wooden form with a central perforation and are sewn on the garment by wrapping threads inserted through this perforation and secured with a decorative knot on the crown of the button.

The preserved length of the front of the coat is 89 cm. The upper limit of the lace is marked by the turning under of the fabric and lining at the end of the lace and there are five horizontal points on each side which end about waist height. They are spaced from the top down as follows: 1.5 cm. between the first and second points; 3 cm. between the second and third and between the third and fourth; 2.5 cm. between the fourth and fifth. The pocket flaps are laced all around the edges and have three buttons. Although there was a seam on the coat body beneath the upper part of the flap, it was sewn shut with the edges abutting and there was no indication of a pocket underneath. The flap is lined and attached to the coat by large stitches at the upper corners and the center. A diagonal strip of lace runs from the front edge of the coat below the fifth point towards the hem and, although the strip was not complete, it probably continued down to the hem. This is most likely a representation of the fold which appeared on many coats.

The complete length of the back was preserved and it is 100 cm. long. The center back seam is sewn flat with the edges abutting and covered with the narrower lace down to the waist, at which point the two parts of the back separate and the single strip of lace expands into two bands to continue down the tails.

The arm hole, shoulder and front sleeve seams are all sewn with the edges abutting and laced. The only seam for which there is little evidence is the back sleeve seam; this was not laced. However, its junction with the armhole can be seen, so it was not difficult to reconstruct. The cuff is large, 21 cm. deep, and the upper edge is 54 cm. in circumference. The upper and front seams of the cuff are laced but the rear seam is plain. The cuff has two vertical points, each with two buttons, and is lined; the lining is turned under in a 1 cm. deep hem and has but one seam (*Margaret Kimball Brown* 1971: Total).

The coat was determined to be of French origin. The style is not that of civilian dress, but of military uniforms of the mid-18th century. It was made based on that military style for exclusive use in the Indian trade. Records indicate that the popular colors were blue, red and yellow; in combination with the lace which would have been a shiny yellow brass when new. The coat was probably worth 14 heavy deerskins or 21 light ones.

MATCHCOAT or BLANKET STROUD

Mid-18th century paintings reveal the use of the stroud or "Matchcoat" from the Powhatan dialect of the Algonquin language "*Matshcore*." This is a mantle or similar loose covering of furs, feathers or woolen cloth often worn over one shoulder and wrapped around the waist somewhat in the manner of a Roman toga. This cape was often embellished with rows of solid color ribbons as illustrated in a 1780 painting of Sir John Caldwell (*Brasser* 1976: Cover Plate).

This type of cape or matchcoat, illustrated in *Fig-*

WARRIOR IN BATTLE
1740 - 1790

HAIR - plucked out except for several scalplocks, two of which are decorated with wrapped porcupine quills, a third decorated with silver brooches. Hawk feathers were tied into the remaining tuft of hair for further embellishment

TATTOOS - Permanent markings of zigzag lines and mythological figures adorn the head, chest and stomach of a spiritually guided warrior

DISTENDED EAR LOBES - Wrapped with earwires, and embellished with a silver cross of Lorraine and a captured trophy of battle - a Gold Watch

MILITARY COAT - Captured in battle off of a soldier who didn't need it anymore, the warrior wears it with pride as a symbol of his accomplishments

NOSE RING - Silver rings were positioned through the septum and worn as a sign of masculinity

QUILLED BAG - Hunting bags were often made from elk or moose hide and dyed with walnut hulls to create a dark color and embellished with appliqued quillwork - symbols of the guiding spirits and manitos of tribal affiliation

POWDER HORN - Scrimshaw done extensively on a necessary item carried into battle to be used with the trade rifle

BREECHCLOUT - Blue or red stroud cloth edged with silk ribbon and silver brooches worn beneath the military coat

LEGGINGS - Deerskin with center seam leggings held in place with leather thongs tied to the waist band holding the clout. Slightly fringed at the ankle, the leggings fit over the top of the moccasins

MOCCASINS - Plain center seam style moccasins protect the wearer in battle as he tracks his enemy

SCALP - With a knife still in hand, a scalp drips fresh blood as a symbol of the warrior's recent victory

FIGURE 79

FIGURE 79

WARRIOR AT PEACE
1745 - 1790

Tribal negotiations often included the use of a wampum belt to symbolize friendship, peace, brotherhood among tribes, etc. As the French and the British fought for control of the many lands still held by the Indians, tribes formed alliances with traditionally unfriendly villages to make stronger armies to fight the Europeans that threatened their very way of life. Pontiac was one of those leaders that was able to make a strong confederacy as he passed the belt of unification among the neighboring Ottawa, Chippewa, Menominee, Algonkian and Miami, among others, in his quest to aid the French hold on the fur trade in the Great Lakes.

HEADGEAR - Porcupine guard hair roach tied to the scalplock, surrounded by an otter fur turban and finally embellished with a silver crown

EARS - Distended ear lobes that had been pierced to contain a multitude of ball and cone ear bobs

FACE - The black stripes of the warrior symbolize his past successful triumphs in battle

NECKLACES - Made from glass trade beads from Italy. These were white heart beads with yellow centers, chevrons and blue facetted Russian beads surrounded by a brass gorget - a trophy of battle

MATCHCOAT - Draped over one shoulder and fastened at the waist is a ribbon decorated cape. Ribbons of the same or of contrasting colors were often sewn in rows covering nearly one third of the blanket leaving only a fraction of an inch between ribbons

BREECHCLOUT - This is short in length and edged with white beads

LEGGINGS - Made of elk skin, they are fitted tightly to each leg and held in place with leather thongs extending up to the waist and tied

GARTERS - Finger-woven wool garters with white beads woven in a diagonal pattern, and edged with silver cones and otter or mink tabs positioned over the knee cap

MOCCASINS - Split elk skin, center-seam moccasins with a round inset that is quilled. The flaps are plain except for edge beading

FIGURE 80

FIGURE 80

MATCHCOAT

Early 18th century Indian women were often issued a stroud or blanket which was used as a cover, often draped over one shoulder and fastened in front with a blanket pin or at the waist with a sash. This was often referred to as a matchcoat worn over a wool stroud wrapped skirt or petticoat.

BLANKET - White was the most common color but red, blue and green were also common.

SHIRT - Wool stroud or duffle cloth wrapped around the waist and held in place with a sash and hangs to just below the knee.

LEGGINGS - In summer, they were worn from below the knee tight around the leg and made to fit into the moccasin. In winter, tied with a garter above the knee and fitted to the leg and tucked into the moccasins with flaps tied up around the ankle.

MOCCASINS - A single piece of split elk, moose, buffalo or deer hide was used to make these center seam moccasins with wing flaps. In winter they were stuffed with a rabbit skin liner, moss or cattail fluffs.

EARBOB - Single silver ball and cone. Shorter cones were used early in the fur trade.

HAIR - Tied back in a single braid and tucked into a quilled hair wrap.

The blanket was draped in soft folds as it wraps around the woman's body and at times it was used to hold a baby or to carry other belongings.

At this early period of the trade (1680-1760), Indian women often wore a matchcoat in place of the shirt or fitted jacket that was to be seen later.

FIGURE 81

FIGURE 81

FIGURE 82

ures 81 and *82*, was listed on very early trade lists. In 1755, a description from Fort Cumberland of the Indians who were to aid Braddock states that their main article of clothing was a blanket or coat, which was thrown around the shoulders (*Sargent*: p. 373). For protection against the winter snow of 1747, the Pennsylvania government sent matchcoats, strouds, blankets, powder and lead to keep certain Indian "friends" of the colony alive (*Jacobs* 1967: p. 97). At the death of Shamokin, a Mohawk friend of the Pennsylvania Assembly in 1749, strouds, matchcoats, wampum, shirts, and "sundry small things were sent to his children and grandchildren to indicate the sorrow of the Quaker province (*Pennsylvania Archives II*: pp. 23-24).

The women also wore this matchcoat over a skirt and trade shirts. Often, rows of silk ribbons are placed across the blanket nearly covering it up to the waist leaving only a fine strip of wool showing between each ribbon (*Brasser* 1976: Front).

BLANKET COATS or CAPOTES

Blanket coats show up in the early 19th century paintings and in the records of the late 18th century. Predominant colors include the early Witney and Hudson's Bay white with blue or black solid stripes. All of the colors were available in the late 18th century with the candy-stripe being introduced in the 19th century. The basic style of the blanket coat included loosely-fitted sleeves that often turned over at the wrist forming a cuff, pointed hood attached or detached and a belt of the same fabric. Blankets were often wrapped around the women, covering the entire body and held in place in front just under the chin with a blanket pin. In the early 19th century (*circa* 1830), we have fairly concrete evidence of silk ribbon applique being done on the hem and inside the front sides of the blanket (*Winter Painting* 1838).

Men sometimes wore blankets over one shoulder and under the opposite arm, the lower part of the blanket being drawn closely around the waist. The blanket worn in this manner provided for freedom of movement with both arms. Women usually wore the blanket wrapped around the lower half of the body like a tight skirt and fastened with a sash at the waist. The upper part of the blanket was then thrown loosely around the arms and shoulders, affording warmth and yet leaving the arms free for work. A woman could carry her baby in the blanket between her shoulders after it was too big for the cradleboard (*Winter* 1948: pp. 209-210).

Usable remnants of old blankets were used to make clothing for the children; coats, pointed hoods and socks that were worn inside of the winter moccasins. Old blankets were raveled to make yarn for weaving bags and sashes. A thin, threadbare blanket was used to strain maple sap and remove twigs and bark before the sap was boiled.

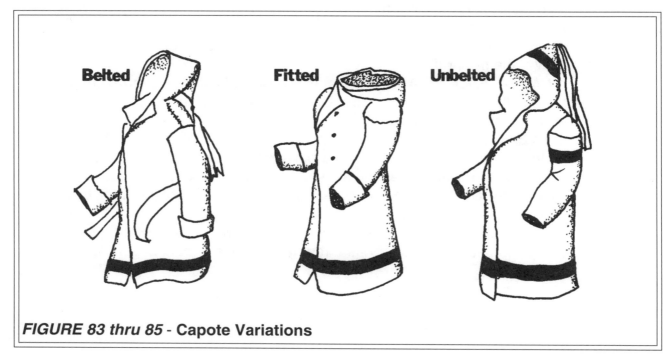

Belted   **Fitted**   **Unbelted**

FIGURE 83 thru 85 - **Capote Variations**

INDIAN MEN
1790 - 1845

After 1795, a warrior's status changed considerably in the Great Lakes region. Peace was at hand for the most part due to the lack of unity among the tribes which had forced them into many battles during the past century thus opposing each other in addition to the invading enemy. Exceptions did occur during the first decade of the 19th century with the War of 1812 through the time of Blackhawk's War in the 1830s. The majority of the "warriors" had turned to keeping the peace and acquiring goods distributed by government factors and agents stationed at Fort Wayne, Detroit, Dearborn and other outposts in the Old Northwest Territory.

HAIR - No longer plucked or shaved. Instead it was left to grow shoulder length and often was covered with colorful headgear

SILK TURBANS - A length of silk wrapped around a man's head and tied so that the remaining silk trails down the back

SILVER CROWNS - Highly polished silver bands often were made and fitted over the silk turban giving the warrior the appearance of royalty

FUR TURBAN - Otter or beaver pelts were often made into fitted caps or turbans that were worn alone or, as in this case, resting just beneath the silver crown over the silk turban

OSTRICH PLUMES - Embellishments for turbans tucked into the folds of the cloth

EAR WHEELS - Silver cut-out wheels in graduated sizes hang from each ear

TRADE SHIRT - Although unseen for the most part in this view, this was a vital part of the male ensemble

SILK CRAVAT - The silk cravat is tied around the collar of the shirt hanging over the front ruffle of the shirt

HUNTING FROCK - A blue linen hunting frock with double layers of fringe was worn over the linen or calico trade shirt. This was embellished with silver ring brooches and engraved silver arm bands

SILVER GORGETS - Crescent-shaped, concave silver pieces were often issued to the Indians as a symbol of a warrior's feats in battle. Some believe it was a symbol of the altar utilized by many of the Algonquin speaking tribes

FINGER-WOVEN SASH - Wrapped over the shoulder of the frock coat and around the waist and tied in place on the side

WAR CLUB - Gunstock war club is decorated with paint, brass buttons, and steel spikes used symbolically as a remnant of days of battles gone by

FIGURE 86

FIGURE 86

Use a 70" x 90" blanket; a larger blanket will allow for more additions to the basic capote such as a cape or stand-up collar, fringe at the shoulders or hood ties. Before cutting the blanket, cut a paper pattern to these dimensions (below) and position on blanket, cut and then follow this sequence:

1. Sew sleeves and body (side and shoulder seams first)
2. Sew rear of hood together
3. Join hood to body; join sleeves to body
4. Cape or collar added at same time the hood is sewn on
5. Add belt loops if desired and attach belt to center back
6. Add hood ties to top of seam in back

Pattern may be modified to accommodate a sash 3" wide from the blanket length.

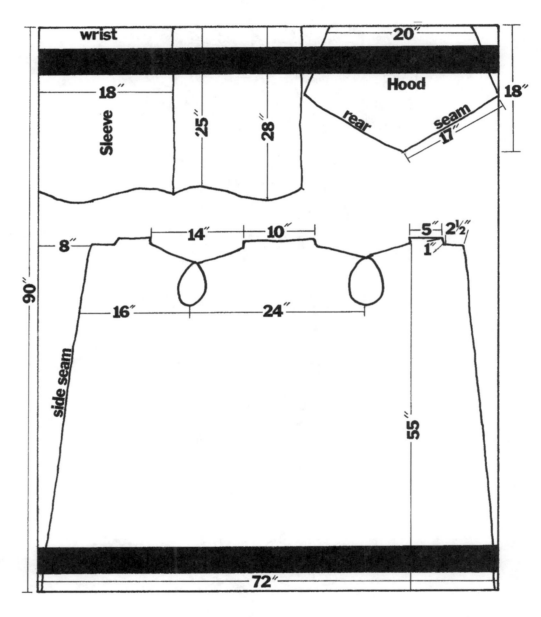

FIGURE 87
CAPOTE PATTERN

110

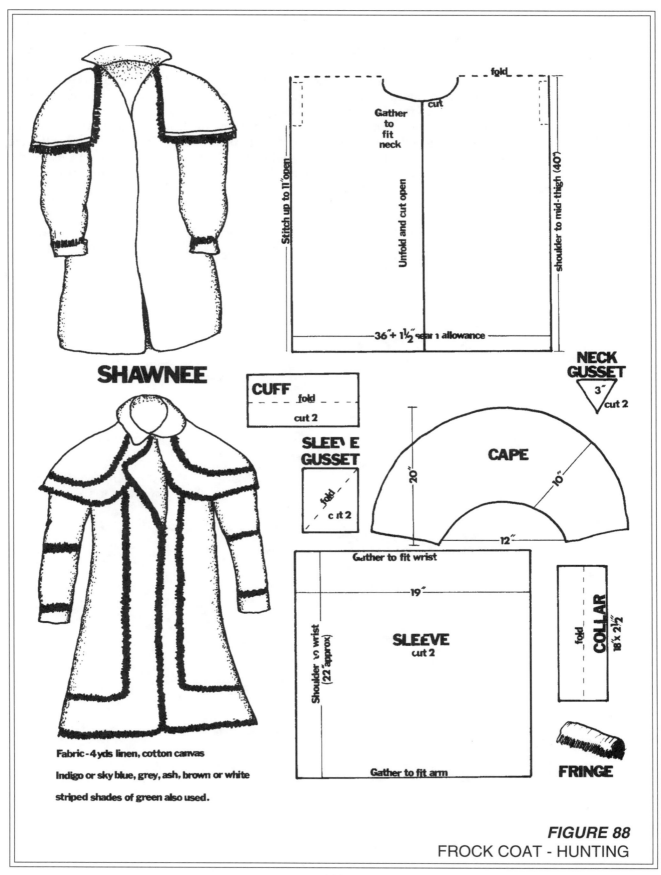

SHAWNEE

Gather to fit neck

Stitch up to 11″ open

Unfold and cut open

fold

cut

shoulder to mid-thigh (40″)

36″ + 1½″ seam allowance

NECK GUSSET 3″ cut 2

CUFF fold cut 2

SLEEVE GUSSET fold cut 2

CAPE 20″ 10″ 12″

Gather to fit wrist

19″

Shoulder to wrist (22″ approx)

SLEEVE cut 2

Gather to fit arm

COLLAR fold 18″ x 2½″

FRINGE

Fabric - 4 yds linen, cotton canvas

Indigo or sky blue, grey, ash, brown or white

striped shades of green also used.

FIGURE 88
FROCK COAT - HUNTING

During and after the Revolutionary War Period, linen hunting frocks were given in trade and as gifts to Indian men and the hunting frock appears frequently in paintings of the early 19th century. It was worn as an outer garment over a trade shirt and embellished with silver brooches, finger-woven sash and bandolier bag.

The hunting frock was seen in several styles and colors. Some frocks had more than one cape which were often self-fringed. Favorite colors were blue, brown, white, and white or beige with red or other contrasting vertical stripes.

The caped-hunting frock seems to have influenced the style of shirts worn by Indian women during the late 18th and early 19th centuries. The large cape of the hunting frock was copied and attached to the trade shirts worn by women from Quebec to Wisconsin.

AUTHOR'S POST SCRIPT

WHAT DID THEY REALLY LOOK LIKE

Many students have conducted powwows or plays where they attempted to dress up as "Indians." The stereotypical image of the Native American has given rise to the concept of all Native American males wearing long fringed buckskins with woven beadwork attached, large feathered war bonnets, doing a war dance with stone tomahawks in their hands. The same could be said of the image of the Native American women who are depicted as "princesses" with the typical "T" style skin dresses and their hair in long braids crowned with feathered headbands and proverbial knee high buckskin boots.

This image, though seemingly universal, is to say the least inaccurate and actually an insult to Native American people. In reality, each Tribe or each region had very specific clothing styles, different perhaps from other tribes living in the same general area based partly upon environmental factors, availability of materials, ritual behavior and, more precisely, based on the culture in which the people lived.

How did this image which stereotypes the vast array of Native Americans come about? In truth, many factors played a part in fixing a biased image of Native Americans, not the least of which were the Native Americans themselves. Explorers, traders and missionaries who first visited the shores of the North American continent were ultimately followed by military regiments from all over Europe. These were the Europeans to have the most contact with the original inhabitants of this land. A few images were put on canvas, highlighting dramatic events or spectacular images of the few Natives Americans that they saw. Since photography had not been invented, the images that Europeans had of these "savages" were either from oral reports, which were often biased and exaggerated, or the few pictorial renderings that were often influenced by the artist's own ideas.

Often, when the Indian people were painted or sketched, they were put into the background as if they were just part of the overall natural scene and not the focal point of the actual rendering. Canadian artist, George Heriot was responsible for some of the renderings of this type depicting Hurons and other occupants of Native villages in the aforementioned manner in his late 18th and early 19th century works. Some traders, military officers, voyageurs and a few early settlers made a point of "collecting" some souvenirs of their ventures into Indian Territory. Fortunately, many of these items can be found in museums in this country, although many were carried across the sea where they remain today in some of Europe's most prestigious museums.

It wasn't until after the American Revolution, and even some years later, after another series of battles had been fought in the land of the Wabash and Maumee Rivers, that the American government wanted a background study done on some of the Tribes that remained in the Great Lakes Region. This was done because of intertribal disagreements over land holdings to which the government wished to gain access. Therefore, they sent artists along with other government officials to make a "permanent record" of the Indian Nations with which they were dealing. Several artists came to Indiana during this time of the treaty signings between 1795 and 1840, both as representatives of the government as well as individuals who were interested in "capturing" the image of the real "Native Americans." Those artists who concentrated on the Great Lakes Region did so because these were the Tribes involved in land issues with the government. Those east of this region had been dealt with decades earlier in battle, routed or removed and more or less forgotten for the moment.

In the Great Lakes Region, the period between 1820-1850 was the "Removal Period" when tribes were forced to sign treaties, whereby they agreed to give up their land and remove to reservations west of the Mississippi to the new "Indian Territory." Those Tribes, or portions of Tribes, that were allowed to stay behind were assimilated into the dominant culture in order to survive. Although Indiana became a state in 1816, and the surrounding regions became states within a period of 20 years of that year either before Indiana or shortly thereafter, settlement of this region was still quite slow until after the Indians were more or less gone. This is why many local histories begin with their own settlement and negate the history and image of the Indians that lived there long before they did.

By the time of the Gold Rush in the 1840's, the Civil War of the 1860's and the massive migration for cheap land out west, photography became a factor in recording the Indians that were standing between these pioneers and the untamed West. Those Tribes that had been "removed" to lands out west encountered resistance from those that were already living there. In order for the newcomers to survive under hostile conditions, they assimilated into the dominant Native cultures that surrounded them. The Tribes that once called the Woodlands their homes were forced by the domino effect to leave those places and take up a lifestyle that up to now was only associated with the Western Plains and Great Basin: That of the nomadic hunter moving with a more portable structure such as a Tipi rather than living the settled life of their ancestors in the forests surrounding the Great Lakes.

By the end of the 19th century, the Native American was fighting his last battle to withstand the onslaught of the "white man." This race to settle the West made a lasting impression on the naive but determined pioneer. Although there were deadly encounters between these pioneers and the nomads of the prairies, most of what they thought they knew about the Indians or "Injuns" or "savages," as the pioneers called them, came from propaganda reported in eastern big city newspapers to stir up the imagination of the public and, of course, to sell newspapers. How much truth was really in those stories? Much of the truth was smothered with exaggerated tales of savagery, brutality and warfare. These stories in the newspapers became the inspiration for the "Western Novel" which further enhanced the image of the "Savage."

Artists who put the first visual images in print to illustrate these fantastically exaggerated articles drew much from their own imagination. These fairy tale renderings only served to stir others to write more fantastic tales about the inhabitants of the Plains. Some former soldiers who later became "Indian fighters," found that when most of the Natives had been subdued, the feeling of the "Wild West" could not easily be cast aside. Indeed, it was that very image that people back East, and even in Europe, wanted to see. It was far too late for most who made their way west. The buffalo were all but gone, which had been the mainstay of the Plains Indians, and now they were starving for anything - any image of the "Old West." People like Buffalo Bill Cody and Wild Bill (Jim) Hickock decided to keep the image of the Old West alive by forming Wild West shows. These were filled with wild west animals, horse riders, and, of course, "Indians." Some were pulled off reservations and put into fancy war shirts, leggings, breechclout and feathered warbonnets and paid to act like "Wild Indians." These shows were so successful that they took them on the road, first by stage and then by train, to the cities, the country and farm towns. The focal point was the kind of "Plains Indians" that the public wanted to see, whether or not it was even close to reality.

When these "circus" shows traveled east and winter came, instead of shipping the Indians back home, the show often dumped them off with other Indian people, like the Indiana Miami, who were still living along the Wabash. These performers stayed with the local Indians through the winter. Miami children, like many other children, were impressed with these "Wild West Indians" and picked up many ideas, customs and bits and pieces of this Western Culture. The Indians who stayed with such people as the Miami or Cherokee back east often did not even have the money to buy food or pay rent, so they traded their moccasins and "costumes" from the shows to their hosts. Just one case in point being that several items found in the collection of Miami items at the Miami County Museum in Peru, Indiana, were parts of "western costumes" belonging to guests that once stayed with some of the Godfroy family and others.

Many of the tribes that remained in their Native homelands lost their land, language, arts and the knowledge of much of their ritual beliefs. This was because many were forced to attend white schools or schools that only taught practical things for students such as English, reading, farming and taught them to forget their former ways. Sometimes, if they did not comply, punishment was invoked upon the students.

Further, as the still life camera evolved into the motion picture camera, the Wild West shows and the "Savage" image of the Plains Indian was put on film, thus further distorting the real life image by using nonnative actors to play the roles of Indians on horseback chasing the so-called poor pioneers or the heroic soldiers. The Indian, in these productions, became a symbol to the average citizen of how the heroic pioneers tamed the West and "civilized the savage." More movies were made that perpetuated the now "stereotypical Indian." More novels were written and still more myths and misconceptions became the foundation of still more movies, television shows, cartoons and even found their way into classrooms around the world.

Even today, authors write best selling books that take advantage of historical figures by using their names, even describing dates, times and places that certain events in history took place that can be verified or documented. The problem comes in to play when the author surrounds the figures and events in fantasy, fiction and fairy tale and then markets the work as "Historical Narrative" about frontier life. These are marketed on a wide scale and thousands of readers are again induced to believe the written word, and due to their popularity, the public takes this image as gospel, leaving still another distorted image of the Native American.

In the last decade or so there have been fairly good attempts at changing this old image and bringing out more factual information on clothing styles, house types, lifestyle, and in general historical events involving Native Americans. Even Hollywood has realized that people no longer want to have the old stale image drilled into their heads. This was evident when Kevin Costner broke the first barriers with the motion picture *Dances with Wolves* that at last gave a realistic view of the Plains Indians. Perhaps less publicized, but just as vital was the 1992 breakthrough movie about the east called "The Last of the Mohicans." This film gave real Native Americans a chance to portray Eastern

FIGURE 89

Woodland Indians in an authentic setting in authentic clothing. It will not wipe away 200 years of stereotyped images and in some ways still lacks the fine-tuning of realism but it is a start.

Dozens of books have finally begun to be written by Native Americans, knowledgeable anthropologists, historians and researchers. They have found the best way to begin changing the image of the Native American is to educate the public through the written word and video documentaries. Books and documentaries for educational channels are being turned out now that are based on first hand accounts from Native Americans, traders, missionaries, military personnel, archaeological evidence, paintings, trade lists, and ex-captives. They are made using identifiable artifacts found in museums and in the hands of knowledgeable private collectors. What remains behind must be used to its fullest if we are to have more than just a rudimentary understanding of such a great people who gave so much to our American way of life.

WHY WORRY ABOUT STEREOTYPES?

The reason for this dissertation on the "stereotype" of the Native American concerns how we look at ourselves. Students as well as adults judge each other by the way they look and peer pressure is perhaps even more evident today than at any other time in history. Clothing and hairstyles to the Native Americans were far more than a fashion statement or something put on simply for comfort. The Native Americans were concerned with proper etiquette, taboos, respect for age, wisdom, life achievements, marital status, authority, show of force, victory, bravery, etc. all of which can and were exemplified through clothing, decoration of clothing, embellishment with ornaments such as body paint, tattoos, hairstyles, and accouterments such as quillwork bags, trade beads, knife sheaths, ear bobs, hair roaches and so much more.

An excellent publication compiled and edited by James F. O'Neil II called *Their Bearing is Noble and Proud* published in 1995 is a collection of narratives regarding the appearance of Native Americans from 1740-1815. This rare publication offers researchers insights to many first hand accounts of traders journals, ex-captive diaries and eyewitness accounts detailing clothing, adornment, and the general appearance of many Native Americans on the Eastern Frontier. These and other accounts were the types of resources that were drawn upon years ago when the original work was done for this publication. With that said, there is still much more to be accomplished in research and publication concerning the clothing and lifestyles of the woodland people east of the Mississippi River.

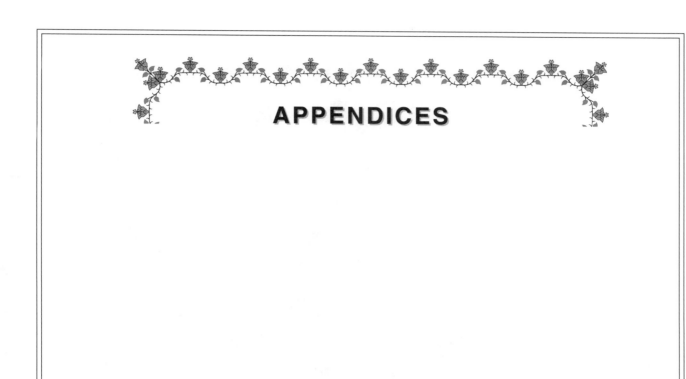

APPENDICES

FIGURE 90 - TATTOOED MAN

Narratives and journals of captives among the tribes of the Great Lakes provide vital information on their mode of dress and customs. By studying several of these accounts, a much clearer picture of Indian clothing can be obtained, much of which has been supported by archaeological evidence, museum artifacts and paintings.

Captive Alexander Henry Among the Chippewa

Alexander Henry was an English trader among the Ojibwa and was placed in the custody of a respected Chippewa named Wawatam: "My hair was cut off, and my head shaved, with the exception of a spot on my crown about twice the diameter of a crownpiece. My face was painted with three or four different colors, some parts of it red, and others black. A shirt was provided for me, painted with vermillion mixed with grease. A large collar of wampum was put around my neck, and another suspended on my breast. Both my arms were decorated with large bands of silver above the elbows, besides several smaller ones on the wrists, and my legs were covered with mitasses, a kind of hose made, as is the fashion, of scarlet cloth. Over all I was to wear a scarlet blanket or mantle, and on my head a large bunch of feathers."

He neglected to mention the probable and very basic breechclout and moccasins. Henry spent a year with Wawatam's family and became very well acquainted with their lifestyle. After a winter of hunting and trapping, he was given a share of the catch and in the spring he used them to purchase items that he needed. His shopping list, in his words, included: "... two shirts, at ten pounds beaver each; a pair of leggings, or pantaloons, of scarlet cloth, which with the ribbon to garnish them fashionably, cost me fifteen pounds of beaver; a blanket, at twenty pounds of beaver ..." (*Bender* 1980: p. 15).

John Long - Captive of the Mohawks says,

"I also made moccasins, or Indian shoes, of deerskins dressed and smoked to make the leather soft and pliable, and worked with porcupine quills and small beads, to which are sometimes suspended hawk bells." He also mentions the use of small metal tinkle cones which were hung in rows on pouches and on moccasin fringe. Heavy wool socks were worn inside the moccasins in the winter and are often listed in trader's stock lists. Long occasionally mentions trading leggings, shirts, cloth, etc. which concurs with other trading reports of the times. He also mentions the supplying of hair-pullers made of coiled brass wire around a wooden core. These were used to pull out almost all body hair except the eyelashes and scalplock.

Long also describes the process of tattooing as mentioned earlier in this book.

James Smith - Captive of the Delaware

After a symbolic cleansing with sand by several young ladies, down at the river, Smith's hair was pulled out by hand, the Indian using ashes to aid his grip. A scalplock was left which was first trimmed with scissors and then divided into three locks, two of which were wrapped in narrow beaded garters and the remainder braided and set with silver brooches. His nose and ears were bored and hung with a nose ornament and earrings. Wearing only a breechclout, he was painted in a way similar to Henry and given a wampum neck band and silver arm and wristbands.

He was given a new ruffled shirt, leggings trimmed with ribbons and beads, beaded and quilled garters additionally trimmed with red-dyed hair, and a pair of moccasins. He was again painted and a bunch of red-dyed feathers were tied upright in his hair. He was also given a strike-a-lite kit contained in a polecat skin, a smoking pipe and tobacco, and a tomahawk.

FIGURE 91

The entire dress of the Dakota female consisted of a coat, skirt, leggings, moccasins and blanket. The coat of a woman was made of about two yards of printed cotton cloth. The sleeves were tight, and it was fitted closely to the body, but was fastened only an inch or two on the breast, the neck being bare and the coat open at the lower end. The skirt was made of broadcloth, the ends being lapped and sewn together, but not across the whole breadth. It was supported at the waist by a girdle, the cloth being doubled under the sash, the outer fold not hanging as low as the inner one. The lower end reached about half way from the knee to the ankle, but was often lower than that; and when the wearer was walking through deep snow, bushes or through grass it was worn shorter.

The leggings of the women were made of red or blue broadcloth, reaching from the knee to the ankle, fastened at the upper end with garters and tucked into the moccasins at the lower.

There was no covering for the heads of females except the blanket. Some had coats for winter made of woolen cloth, and others wore several layers of cotton coats. The blanket, essential though it was, was often seen fastened to their waist or laying near where they might be chopping wood.

Different groups of Dakota dressed slightly different from one another. The skirts worn by the Ihank-townwan (Yankton) women reached to their arms and were supported by shoulder straps, leaving their arms bare. Among the northern bands, the women wore leather garments instead of cloth.

The blankets referred to were made of fine blue cloth, heavily and tastefully adorned with silk ribbons of various colors. Some had a band of embroidered work, a foot or more wide, running around the bottom of their skirts, consisting of silk ribbons of diverse colors, folded together and laid in such a manner as to present a variety of figures, with a blending of different colors, among which the more glaring colors, such as red or yellow, by no means predominated.

Besides the embroidery work of ribbons and beads with which they profusely decorated their garments, they wore other ornaments made of silver such as thin, circular plates, two or three inches in diameter, worn on the bosom, often many at once, so that the breast was nearly covered with them. Other items included many strings of beads.

The gala apparel just described was worn by the aristocracy and used only for ceremonies, and assembly meetings. Some of the Dakota women were destitute, not only of ornaments, but of comfortable clothing. All wore plain garments when about their ordinary business, and middle-aged women made little use of ornaments; but the girls would have them if they could get them.

The clothing of the men consisted of a blanket of coarse wool and of dimensions suited to the size of the wearer; for these blankets were made expressly for them. They were generally white, but some were red, green or blue. They preferred white for hunting, believing that the game was less afraid of them.

In summer, the men wore shirts made of cotton, and in winter they wore, over these shirts, coats made of blankets reaching to the knees. The capotes were lapped in front and fastened to keep out the cold.

Their leggings were nearly as long as their legs, and were supported by straps fastened to their girdles. The lower end was made to fit the top of the foot, and being drawn down tight over the moccasin, was fastened by straps which passed under the hollow of the foot. The leggings were made of buckskin in winter, but in wet weather cloth was preferred; and in cold weather both cloth and leather ones might be worn at the same time.

Breechclouts were made of blue wool about a foot wide and three or four feet long. It passed between the legs and under the belt in front and rear, the ends hanging down a foot or more, like an apron, before and behind.

In winter, the men wore hoods made of white blankets, though some of the young men preferred blue broadcloth. The socks, of both men and women, were simply oblong pieces of blanket wrapped around the foot. When expecting to walk far, they put fine, dry grass in the moccasin under the foot.

Blankets were wrapped around their waists and bound with girdles. The lower end of the blanket, doubled in front, reached about to the knees, and the upper part was wrapped about the head and shoulders, protecting all the upper part of the body and also the hands and face.

Hunters wore very different moccasins from those used for ceremonies. The dress moccasins were garnished with porcupine quills, beads and ribbons. The front of the breechclout, leggings, knife sheath and

FIGURE 92

shot-bag were ornamented with quills, ribbons or beads; but these showy decorations were prized only by the young and were discarded by the middle-aged and old.

Men often cut their hair across the forehead but left the rest long, hanging over their shoulders. The young men often wore braids behind the head and also had several small braids hanging down on each side of the face to which were fastened small brooches and beads.

FIGURE 93

A HISTORY OF FINGERWEAVING
by Dick Carney

Until quite recently it had been assumed that fingerweaving was only done by the Woodland Indians of North America, but the discovery of three fine, well-preserved pre-historic pieces in a cave in Arizona have blown that theory. These pieces were woven from a yarn spun from dog hair and are now on display at Mesa Verde National Park.

Although fingerweaving is considered to be a Native American art, it is also found in other parts of the world. Some beautiful sashes are made by the Indians of Peru, South America. The technique used there is somewhat different than that used in North America and is called Rep braiding. Fingerweaving is also found in the Scandinavian countries, especially among the Laplanders. A fragment was found in a peat bog in Denmark which was dated at around 600 years old. It is my opinion that fingerweaving was brought back to Scandinavia by the Vikings when they returned from the east coast of Canada and New England around a thousand years ago.

I have also learned from Osage friends that, according to their oral history, the art goes back more than 2,000 years and was once practiced by all Indians of North America. It has also been brought to my attention that a piece of fingerweaving was recently discovered in a peat bog in Florida which was dated between six and eight thousand years old.

To my knowledge, no one has ever written a history of fingerweaving as such. Frequent mention of it has been made since the earliest contact between whites and Indians, but with little or no detail. We do know that before yarn was made available by the white settlers, sashes were made of thistle fibers, the inner bark of the basswood tree, dog hair, and buffalo wool. Buffalo wool yarn was sun bleached in varying amounts to produce different shades of brown or reddish brown, then fingerwoven to show the various designs.

The first (sheep) wool yarn sashes were made from trade blankets which were unraveled, then re-spun. Because the blankets were of one color, with a narrow band of selvage on each end of another color, the resulting sashes were the same. The center of the sash was woven using the primary color of the blanket and very narrow borders were woven down each side with the yarn from the selvage. White beads were generally woven into both the center portion of the sash and into the borders to form designs such as diamonds, chevrons, parallelograms, zigzag, etc.

As more and varied colors of wool yarn became available, the older technique was slowly abandoned and the different colors were used to produce the designs. White pony beads were still used in many sashes to outline the designs, especially the "arrow" and the "chevron" patterns.

During the last half of the 18th century, the French Canadians learned fingerweaving from the Indians and produced some of the finest examples of the art ever accomplished. These came to be known as the "Assomption" Sashes; so called, because most of them were made in Assomption, Quebec. The yarn used was a wool crewel yarn, which was re-spun. The threads were very small and very tight. The resulting sashes were real masterpieces varying in width from 5" to more than 15". Many were over fifteen feet in length. They were sold to an agent or broker who, in turn, sold them to the Hudson's Bay Company or the Northwest Trade Company for resale. They became the trademark of the voyageurs, who wore them both because it gave them prestige when dealing with the Indians and because they thought it would keep them from getting hernias while carrying huge bundles of furs. The latter belief was ill founded and death from strangulated hernias was the fate of many voyageurs.

Around 1830, the design and colors of the Assomption sash was standardized for the Hudson's Bay Company. A few years later the weavers went on strike for more pay. The HBC's answer to the strike was to produce a machine-made copy in England and this effectively ended the fingerweaving industry of Assomption.

By the time I learned fingerweaving in 1960, it had almost become a lost art. Since then, there has been a revival of interest, due in large part to the craft revivals among some of the Indian tribes, especially the Osage, and to the growing interest in history centered among the black-powder rendezvous folks.

I have taught fingerweaving to over a hundred people and was told by an Osage lady named Maudie Cheshewalla, that she has taught more than 600 Osage. I am delighted to see so much interest in the art and to see so many talented weavers evolving.

Editor's Note: Recently it has been noted by the editor and other scholars, that fingerweaving has not "almost become a lost art" among many of the tribes that were originally found in the Great Lakes Region.

Fine examples of the finger-woven sash may be observed at the contemporary gatherings of the Ojibwa, Kickapoo, Winnebago and others, and these skills have been passed from grandmother to granddaughter through the ages. Further, whether by tradition or from the proximity of the Nebraska band of the Winnebago Tribe, women of the Omaha now produce some fine finger-woven articles.

FINGERWEAVING
by Mae Ring

Fingerweaving began in prehistoric times when Natives in North America utilized various plant fibers to weave bags, sashes and bands, remnants of which have been found in archaeological digs. Historically, sashes of wool, and of wool and glass beads woven throughout, were made and used by the Indians of the Great Lakes and Eastern colonies in the 18th and early 19th centuries.

Index of terms that will be useful: *Shed* is the space you have made by separating upper and lower strands; *Warp* is the portion of strands that hang vertical; *Weft* is the portion of strand used in the shed (horizontal); and, *Selvage* is the edge on either side of the weaving.

In order to get started, I recommend plant fibers (rug yarn); cotton doesn't stretch as much as an animal fibre. Most commercial yarns contain acrylics (synthetic textile) which makes a fairly stable weave.

Your first project will be the diagonal pattern, see *Figure 94*. Select five colors of your choice avoiding black and very dark colors on this project because they are hard to see in artificial light.

Determine the length you will need for the warp threads by adding your waist measurement, the length of the fringe and knot needed to tie sash and then add 1/2 of this figure to give needed length.

Then tie one end of the warp threads to a secure object, such as a chair, and loop each strand once around a "head stick," as shown in *Figure 93*. If you center your stick, you will have a shorter length of strands to work through. Most patterns can be worked this way.

As close to the looped head stick as possible, twine every two strands parallel to the stick. This will help keep the strands separated and give easier control. On the chair, keep the secured untwined end at a height that is comfortable for you to weave and still maintain tension.

Your second project should be a chevron (see *Figure 95*) which is a double diagonal pattern. Your third project should be a diamond which is a reversed chevron. You now should have good tension control.

The lightning pattern (*Figure 96*) when doubled is the flechette or dart design.

You now have the basic knowledge to create infinite patterns. May you have many years of weaving pleasure and satisfaction as you grow from pattern to pattern.

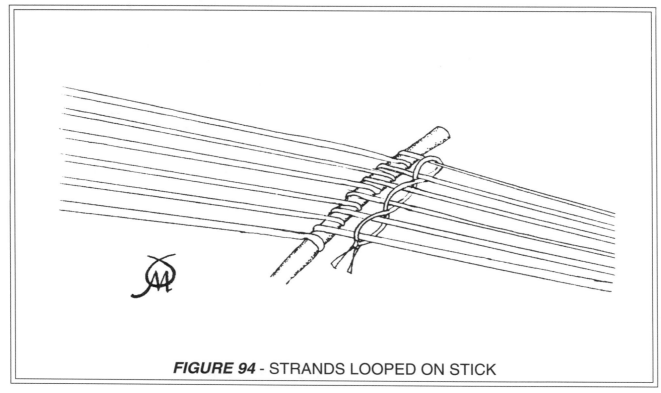

FIGURE 94 - STRANDS LOOPED ON STICK

FIGURE 95 - DIAGONAL PATTERN

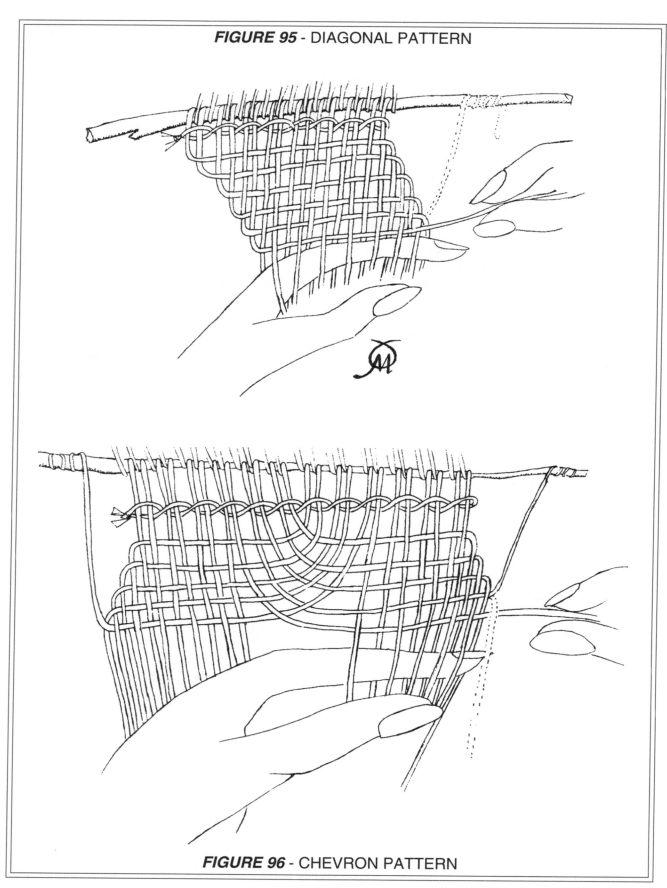

FIGURE 96 - CHEVRON PATTERN

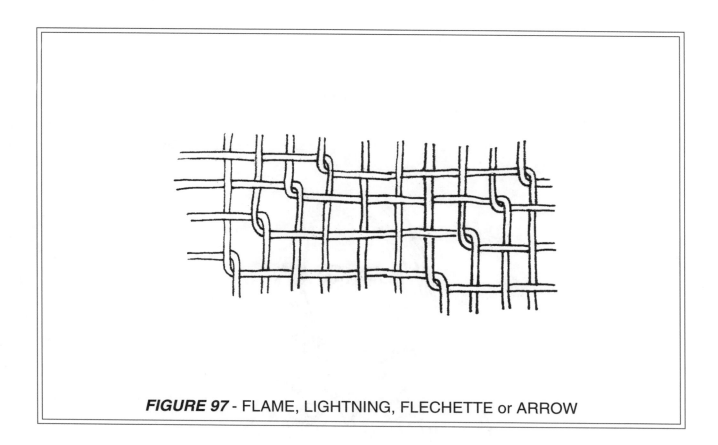

FIGURE 97 - FLAME, LIGHTNING, FLECHETTE or ARROW

FIGURE 98 - LaBLONDE WITH TRADE SILVER ADORNMENT

Trading for silver began in the 1500s with the Native Americans and the then-seasoned fishing boats coming from the British Isles. The crew members of these boats traded their personal items, such as clock brooches, Luckenbooth pins, crosses and Masonic pins to the inhabitants of the New World for whatever the natives had to offer; mainly fur pelts. These silver pieces coming from across the Atlantic were high quality, finely detailed pieces of sterling silver, made by British smiths.

The four predominant shapes appealed to the natives and became the focus of the developing silver trade, which grew slowly until about 1725. The designs changed slightly over the years and the cross and Masonic brooch gradually lost their religious significance. A fifth item emerged which greatly appealed to the Native Americans; the ball and cone earring. Even though there were many other styles of trade silver, these five major types prevailed.

Since the wearing of one's wealth is highly esteemed in primitive cultures and silver was also easily spendable, it was common for the natives (and those whites in contact with them) to wear hundreds of brooches in any fashion or pattern to decorate their clothing. A tongue-like fastener secured the brooch to the cloth so the silver could be easily removed, if necessary, for trade. Even the earrings were worn in multiples, not only in the ears, but also hung on the brooches to make a kind of bell which jingled.

From 1725 until about 1825, silver was one of the dominant items of the fur trade. During this period high quality trade pieces were being manufactured by white smiths in Montreal, Detroit, Philadelphia, etc. These early craftsmen used hand-made iron punches or chisels which were driven through the metal into end-grained wood, domed by hammering the silver on a polished iron block, filed, polished, and lastly, engraved. The predominant material was still silver, which was readily available from coins.

Toward the end of this period, the beaver population was being depleted in the Old Northwest and trappers were moving west of the Mississippi River to obtain the pelts. With the traders gone, the Indian himself began making silver pieces, but used slightly different methods of construction. The pattern was transferred to the metal by scratching, then sawed out. If doming was done, the silver was laid into a spherically cupped wooden block and hammered. With this method there was very little need for filing and most of the Indian pieces were considered "finished" at this crude stage.

The most common material used by the Indians was a silver-colored metal called German silver. This metal consists of an alloy of nickle, copper and zinc. It contains no silver, but has a shiny surface. Although German silver came into this country about 1825, this material was not readily obtainable at the trading posts until after 1850.

Arm bands, bracelets, gorgets, finger rings and hat bands added to the list of trade silver items, but the five most popular shapes flourished throughout the entire trade period.

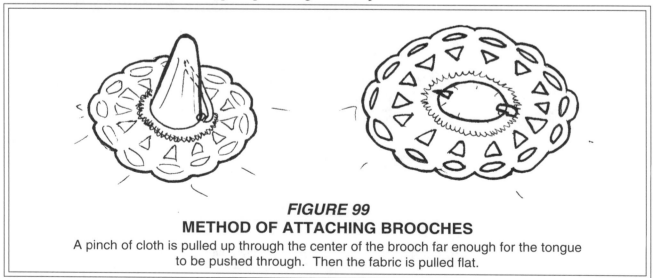

FIGURE 99
METHOD OF ATTACHING BROOCHES
A pinch of cloth is pulled up through the center of the brooch far enough for the tongue to be pushed through. Then the fabric is pulled flat.

**Luckenbooth or
Double Heart Brooch**

**Cloak Brooch or
Round Brooch**

**Ball & Cone
Earring**

**Cross of Lorraine
or
Double Bar Cross**

**Masonic Brooch
or
Council Fire Brooch**

FIGURE 100 - TRADE SILVER EXAMPLES

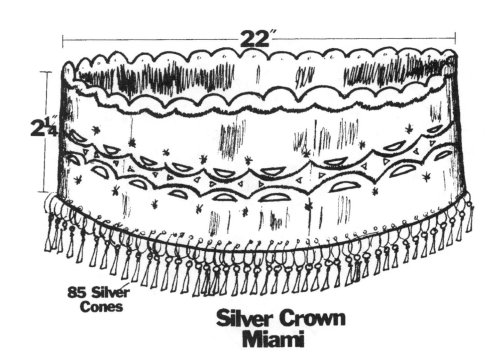

22″

2¼″

85 Silver
Cones

**Silver Crown
Miami**

⅜″

**Ring
Brooch**

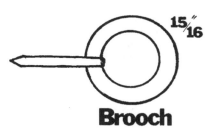

15/16″

Brooch

1½″

**Silver
Brooch**

FIGURE 101 - TRADE SILVER EXAMPLES
Source: Miami County Museum, Peru, Indiana
Author: Director of Education

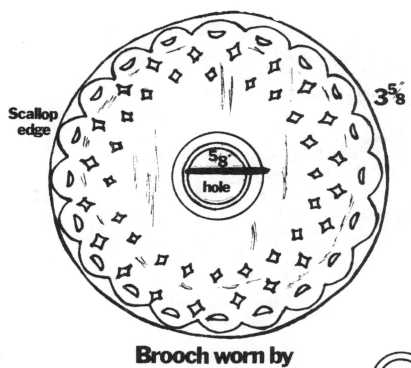

Scallop
edge

$3\frac{5}{8}''$

$\frac{5}{8}''$
hole

**Brooch worn by
"Shingo" Miami**

**Silver
Button**

$\frac{3}{4}''$

**Ring
Brooch**

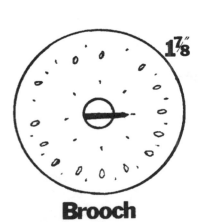

$1\frac{7}{8}''$

Brooch

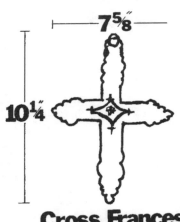

$7\frac{5}{8}''$

$10\frac{1}{4}''$

**Cross Frances
Slocum Miami**

FIGURE 102 - TRADE SILVER EXAMPLES
Source: Miami County Museum, Peru, Indiana
Author: Director of Education

GLOSSARY OF CLOTHING AND EMBELLISHMENT TERMS USED IN THIS BOOK:

ATASIMA - Miami word for a pair of leggings

BREECHCLOUT - Cloth or leather garment worn by Indian men and some women passing between the legs and held in place at the waist with a sash allowing extended length of garment to fall down the front and back of the wearer.

CALICO - A cotton fabric used in the 18th century for shirts; often printed with large, flowery designs or overall block print patterns on a plain background; generally any cotton fabric originally imported from India.

CAPOTE - Simple coat made from trade wool blanket material, wrapped around the body and tied at the waist with a sash; has sewn in sleeves, pointed hood (sometimes detached), and fastened in front with button or a sash.

CLOCK - Bell-shaped embroidered or woven ornament on a sock or stocking going up the ankle.

COATS - Military style trade coats were made specifically to trade to the Indians, often made of wool and decorated with gaudy lace, buttons and trim.

DISTENDED EAR LOBES - Indian men often cut the outer 1/4 inch of the ear lobe and pulled it out by placing a small roll of birch bark in the opening. When it was healed the men often wrapped it with ear wires, and pierced the remaining ear to attach wampum beads, silver cones or other ear bobs.

GARTER - Finger-woven sash, leather strap or hand-woven sash used to hold stockings or leggings in place.

HAIRBOW - Hourglass-shaped leather or rawhide covered with trade wool or leather, decorated with edge beads, ribbons and silver buttons used by the Huron, Miami, Delaware, Potawatomi, Shawnee, Kickapoo and others in the Great Lakes as a hair ornament tied to the top of the single braid at the back of the neck. Silk ribbons were sometimes attached and hung down the back of the women's ensemble.

LEGGINGS - Tube-shaped fabric used for covering the leg and commonly held in place with garters. Women usually wore leggings up to the knees in good weather and over the knees in winter. Men used one-half of the width of stroud wool to make each legging, thus creating a pair of leggings that rested just above the knee until better quality and larger blankets were issued toward the end of the 18th century.

MATCHCOAT - From the Powhatan dialect of the Algonquin language "matshcore" which is a mantle of similar loose covering of furs, feathers or woolen cloth often worn over one shoulder and wrapped around the waist somewhat in the manner of a Roman toga.

METACOSHEE - Miami word for petticoat or skirt used by women consisting of a piece of fabric about 60 inches wide and 36 inches long and wrapped around the waist, overlapping one side over the other and held in place with a sash.

NLAPKAKANI - Miami word for skirt.

QUILLWORK - Application of quills in a variety of methods to such things as leggings, moccasins, bags and pouches and knife sheaths. Used extensively in the 18th century among the Great Lakes tribes.

PESMOKIN - Potawatomi word meaning shirt.

RIBBONWORK - Silk ribbons applied in single strips to clothing such as breechclout, moccasins, leggings, skirts and blankets until 1800 when cut-work applique begins to appear on the same creating designs such as diamonds, triangles and other geometric patterns.

SCALPLOCK - The remaining tufts of hair left on the crown of the head after the rest had been plucked or shaved. This is often braided and decorated with brooches, quills and feathers.

SHIRT - Indians were issued fabric and finished shirts during the 18th century made in the then current square-cut fashion and were worn by both Indian men and women. Caped shirts began to be seen after the Revolutionary War Period worn by Indian women.

SILVER BROOCH - A kind of round silver buckle with a tongue, which the Indians fasten to their shirts, leggings, blankets and breechclouts; fastened in rows, at a distance of about the breadth of a finger from one another.

STOCKINGS - Military issue hose of cotton fabric were issued to the Indians and worn by both men and women, held in place with garters.

STROUD - Cheap cloth made of woolen rages, made in Stroudwater, England, usually in red or blue. It was used for blankets, breechclouts, leggings, petticoats and coats.

TURBANS - Silk scarf or finger-woven sash wrapped around the head and used as a decorative head covering.

WAISTCOATS - Vest-type of garment prized by Indian men made of elaborate green, scarlet or blue silk or wool. They were included on trade lists of the 18th century.

WAMPUM - Purple beads made from quahog shell and white beads made from the conch shell strung into necklaces, woven into belts, collars and girdles and traded as far west as the Dakotas. They were used basically in communication of treaties, agreements, and to signify war, peace or friendship according to the design woven into the belt.

GLOSSARY OF FABRIC TERMS USED IN THE FUR TRADE

ALAMODE - Fine, light glossy silk

ALLAPINE - An expensive strong woolen stuff

BAIZE - A cheap, coarse, woolen cloth which was made in several colors

BATISTE - Coarsely woven fine white linen

BIRDSEYE - A silk fabric with light spots on a dark background

BROADCLOTH - A fine, smooth woolen cloth

BROCADE - Silk fabric with raised patterns in varied colors

BUCKSKIN - Made of deer hide

BUFF - Leather made from buffalo skin

CALICO - Printed cotton fabric originally from India with large flowery prints. Any cotton fabric plain white or colors.

CALIMANCO - A woolen textile, plain, striped or checkered and glazed. In the 18th century it was single worsted or glazed. Flanders wool product woven with satin twill, enabling the observer to see checks on one side only.

CAMBRIC - Fine French linen

CAMELOT - Kind of fabric made from silk and camels hair originally; now made with wool and silk. Used for cloaks and petticoats.

CANVAS - Coarse, woven cloth of hemp or flax; used for sails, breeches and jackets; traded to Indians and used on structures

CASTOR - Originally, a beaver pelt from which hats were made; later, a cheaper felt mixed with wool.

CHINTZ - Calico with colored pattern, painted or printed

CORDUROY - 18th century, a thick corded cotton with pile-like velvet

CRAPE - A thin transparent crimped silk gauze

CUTTANEE - A fine East Indian linen used for shirts and cravats

DAMASK - Linen or silk woven in a manner invented in Damascus with a texture with regular features.

DIAPER - Linen cloth woven in flowers and figures

DROGGET - Woolen fabric used for making coats and jackets; formerly a woolen or mixed stuff for clothing

DUCK - Strong, white linen fabric without a twill

DUFFELS - Woolen fabric with a thick tufted or knotted nap. Used to make matchcoats. Originally made in Duffel, England

EVERLASTING - Worsted woolen resembling serge

FEARNAUGHT - A thick cloth with long pile used for making coats and thick winter jackets.

136

FIGURE 103

FELT - Cloth made of wool united without weaving. A solid composition of wool fibers and the hair matted together with heat, moisture and pressure; much used for making hats

FERRET - A kind of narrow riband. A narrow ribbon or tape of cotton or silk

FRIEZE - A coarse warm cloth; wool worn by poor folk

FUSTIAN - A kind of cloth made of linen and cotton; coarse twilled textile with a linen warp and cotton weft with a surface resembling velvet used for jackets and petticoats

FULLED CLOTH - Wool shrunk by wetting and beating

GARLIX - A linen fabric

GAUZE - Thin, transparent silk or linen

GIMP - Silk worsted or cotton twist with cord or wire running through, used for trim

HALFTHICK - Kind of coarse woolen cloth made in Lancashire made into trade coats and blankets for the Indian trade

HEMP - A fibrous plant of which coarse linen and rope are made

HOLLAND - A fine linen made in Holland

JACONET - Soft muslin

KERSEY - Woolen cloth usually coarse and ribbed with cotton warp. Originally from Kersey, England

LIMBOURG - Red or blue fabric from the Netherlands

LINEN - Durable fabric made from weaving flax

LINSEYWOOLSEY - Made of linen and wool

MATCHCOAT - The name given to a coarse woolen cloth used for these coats, but they were chiefly made from Duffels

MAZAMET - Wool for coats similar to Molleton, woven in France

MOLLETON or MOLTON - Wool made in Molton, England

MUSLIN - A fine stuff made of cotton having a downy nap

NANKEEN - Cotton fabric of a yellow-brown color, originally from Nankin, China often made into waistcoats and breeches

OZNABRUG - Cheap and coarse strong linen made in Germany used for sheets, breeches and jackets

RATTEEN - Thick twilled woolen cloth with curled nap used for coats and blankets

RUSSIAN SHEETING - Fabric used for shirts

SAGATHY - Woolen fabric or kind of serge sometimes mixed with silk and used for men's garments

SATIN - A soft shiny twilled silk textile and dull of backside

SERGE - Loosely woven twilled worsted fabric, usually wool

SILK - Product of the silkworm

STROUD - Coarse, cheap woolen cloth made in Stroudwater, England, with undyed selvages used for leggings, blankets, skirts and matchcoats by the Indians

SWANSKIN - Cheap fleecy cloth similar to light flannel used in making waistcoats and lining clothing

TAFFETA - Fine smooth silk with gloss

TIFFANY - Very thin silk gauze

VELVET - Silk with short fur or pile upon it

WHITNEY - A heavy coarse cloth, generally scarlet and used for coats, jackets, petticoats, breeches and cloaks

WOOL - Fleece of sheep woven into cloth of varying grades

WOOLENS - Product made from short-stapled wool

WORSTED - Cloth made of long-stapled wool combed straight and smooth before spinning; originally made in Worsted, England

BIBLIOGRAPHY

American Fur Company, *Michilimachinac Account Book 1821-23*. Chicago Historical Society

Bacqueville de la Potherie, Claude Charles Le Roy, Sier de 1911 *"History of the Savage People who are Allies of New France"* in Indian Tribes of the Upper Mississippi Valley and the Region of the Great Lakes, ed. E. H. Blair

Beckman, Jane. *"Techniques of Applique and Cut Ribbon Work"*, unpublished manuscript, 1967

Blair, Emma Helen, ed/trans, *The Indian Tribes of the Upper Mississippi Valley and Region of the Great Lakes as Described by Nicolas Perrot*, Vol. I & II

Brasser, Ted J. *Bo' jou Nee Jee! Profiles of Canadian Indian Art*, National Museum of Man, Ottawa, Canada, 1976
---------- 1975. *"A Basketful of Indian Culture Change"* National Museum of Man
---------- 1982. *"Pleasing the Spirits" Indian Art Around the Great Lakes"*, Ghylen Press

Clark, Rev. D. W., *Life Among the Indians and Historical Incidents* by James Finley, Cincinnati

Conn, Richard. *Robes of White Shell and Sunrise, Personal Decorative Arts of the Native American*, Denver Art Museum

Ewing, Douglas C. *Pleasing the Spirits*, Ghylen Press, 1982

Flint Institute of Arts. *Indian Art of the Great Lakes*, Flint, MI, 1973

Gibbs, Sandra. *The Covenant Chain - Indian Ceremonies and Trade Silver*, The National Museum of Man, Ottawa, Canada, 1980

Good, Mary Elizabeth. *Guebert Site*: An 18th Century Historic Kaskaskia Indian Village in Randolph County, Illinois, Central State Archaeological Societies, Inc., 1972

Gringhuis, Dirk. *Indian Costume at Mackinac*: 17th and 18th Centuries, Mackinac Island State Park Commission, 1972

Heckewelder, John 1876, *"History, Manners, and Customs of the Indian Nations Who Once Inhabited Pennsylvania and the Neighboring States"* New York

Horan, James D. *The McKenney - Hall Portrait Gallery of American Indians*, 1972

Horse Capture, George P., *"Native American Ribbonwork: A Rainbow Tradition,"* 1980

Jacobs, Wilbur R. *Wilderness Politics and Indian Gifts*: The Northern Colonial Frontier, 1748-1763, 1967

Josephy, Alvin M. Jr. *The Boy Artist of Red River*. American Heritage, American Heritage Publishing Company, NY, February 1970

Johnson, Mary M., Forbes, Judy and Delaney, Kathy. *Historic Colonial French Dress*, Quabache Press, 1982

Johnson, William. *The Papers of Sir William Johnson*, Volumes I - IV, NY, 1921

Leech, Polyak and Ritzenthaler *"Art of the Great Lakes Indians"* 1973, Flint Institute of Arts

Lyford, Carrie. *Ojibway Crafts*, R. Schneider Publications

Mainfort, Robert C. Jr. *Indian Social Dynamics in the Period of European Contact*, Fletcher Site Cemetery, Bay County, Michigan, Publication of the Museum, Michigan State University, 1979

Minnesota Historical Society. *Where Two Worlds Meet*: The Great Lakes Fur Trade, 1982

National Gallery of Canada, Ottawa

Ohio Historical Society 1978. *"Scoouwa: James Smith's Indian Captivity Narrative"*

Pannabecker, Rachael, *"Ribbonwork of the Great Lakes Indians: The Material of Acculturation"* Dissertation Ohio State University, 1986

Peterson, Eugene T. *Gentlemen on the Frontier*: A Pictorial Record of the Culture of Michilimachinac, Mackinac Island State Park Commission, 1964

Phelps, Martha. *Frances Slocum, The Lost Sister of Wyoming*, 1906

Ritzenthaler, Robert and Pat. *The Woodland Indians of the Western Great Lakes*, Milwaukee Public Museum

Scott, James. *The Potawatomi, Conquerors of Illinois*, 1981

Stewart, Ty. *Oklahoma Delaware Women's Dance Clothes*, American Indian Crafts and Culture, Special Issue, 1972

Smithsonian, *Kapplers Laws and Treaties*, 1976

Thornbrough, Gayle, ed. *Letter Book of the Indian Agency at Fort Wayne, 1809-1815*, Indiana Historical Society, 1961

Tipton, John. *The Tipton Papers*, Indiana Historical Bureau, 1942

Trigger, Bruce, ed. *Handbook of North American Indians*, Vol. 15, Northeast: Smithsonian, Washington, D.C., 1980

Viola, Herman J. *The Indian Legacy of Charles Bird King, Smithsonian Institution, 1976*

Winger, Otho. *The Frances Slocum Trail*, 1943

Winter, George. *The Journals and Indian Paintings of George Winter, 1837-1839*, Indiana Historical Society, Lakeside Press, Chicago, 1948

MUSEUMS AND LIBRARIES UTILIZED IN PREPARATION FOR THIS BOOK

Angel Mounds Prehistoric Mississippian Mound Site, Evansville, IN

Atztalan State Park - Prehistoric Mound Site, 35 miles from Madison, WI - Report Study

Cherokee Indian Museum, Cherokee, NC

Chicago Field Museum of Natural History, Chicago, IL - Collection of North American Indian Art, 1981-87

Chicago Historical Society Collection, Chicago, IL
Chicago Public Libraries, Chicago, IL

Cranbrook Institute of Arts, Bloomfield Hills, MI - 1985 Collection Study

Detroit Institute of Arts, Detroit, MI - 1985 Collections Study

Father Marquette State Park Museum, St. Ignace, MI

Fort De Baude Museum, St. Ignace, MI - Collections 1987

Fort Ligonier, Ligonier, PA Displays and Collections and contact with Director West

Fort Wayne - Allen County Library, Fort Wayne, IN - Indiana Collection, Reference Section, Microfilm, Microfiche, Genealogy Section, Art Section

Grand Rapids Public Museum, Grand Rapids, MI Displays and Correspondence with Curator of Collections

Harbor Springs Indian Museum, Harbor Springs, MI Collections and Display 1987

Heye Foundation, Museum of the American Indian, Correspondence with Collections and Library, 1987

Historic Fort Wayne, Inc. Fort Wayne, IN 1980-1983 Miami

Huron Indian Museum, St. Ignace, MI 1987

Indian and Local Historic Artifacts Collections; First Person Living History Program

Indianapolis State Museum, Indianapolis, IN; Rotating Display Study

Indian Heritage Museum, Indianapolis, IN

Miami County Museum - Collections and Archives of Miami Indian Historical Artifacts and numerous files on Miami Indian History

Milwaukee Public Museum - Collections and Contact with Dr. Lurie, Anthropology Dept.

Museum of Man, Ottawa, Canada - Collections Study and Correspondence

Newberry Library, Chicago, IL - McKenney-Hall Portrait Collections; Historical Maps

Neville Public Museum, Green Bay, MI - Collections and Archives

Oneida Indian Museum, Depere, WI 1987

Oshkosh Public Museum, Oshkosh, WI - Collections and Contract with Curator

Romeoville Museum, Romeoville, IL - Displays of French Voyageur Documentation and Fur Trade 1986

Wabash County Museum, Wabash, IN - Collections and Archives

Williams County Museum, Montpelier, OH - Ohio Indian Artifacts Collections including reproductions of Caped Blouse of the Potawatomi; original at the Field Museum in Chicago, IL

Wisconsin State Historical Society and Museum, Madison, WI - Displays, Collections and Archival Material Study 1987

UNIVERSITIES CONTACTED IN PREPARATION FOR THIS BOOK

Ball State University - Anthropology Department. Contact: Don Cochran Staff Archaeologist
Indiana University at Fort Wayne and Bloomington - Anthropology Department. Contact: Glen Black Lab Reports
University of Michigan, Ann Arbor - Anthropology Department
Toledo University, Toledo, Ohio - Anthropology. Contact: Dr. Stothers

INDEX

THE ART OF SIMULATING EAGLE FEATHERS

by
Bob Gutierrez

Another coup for Eagle's View and You!! Nobody else has anything like this fantastic new handbook!! It is the <u>only</u> full color, instructional manual which teaches crafters how to create realistic imitation Golden and Bald Eagle feathers that can be legally used in all of their projects. Noted craftsman and educator Bob Gutierrez shares more than 20 years of experience in creating these marvelous works of art. Explanatory photographs and written descriptions of each and every step required, from feather preparation through each step in the painting process are provided. These same techniques can, of course, be used to create simulations of other predatory species, which are also protected by law. Simple tools, easily obtained materials and a desire to create beauty are all that are needed to get the most out of this book. These feathers are perfect for traditional or contemporary Indian arts and crafts projects and may be created for use in headdresses, bustles, roaches, scalp locks, dream catchers, wall hangings and to decorate almost any project. Don't miss out on this unique book!!

ISBN 0-943604-59-1 in paperback - $9.95

AVAILABLE AT DEALERS OR FROM
Eagle's View Publishing Company
6756 North Fork Road
Liberty, Utah 84310
Please include $5.50 per Order for Shipping Charges

Also Available:

Eagle's View Publishing Company Catalog of Books & Patterns	$3.50
Eagle Feather Trading Post Annotated Catalog of Books	$4.00
Eagle Feather Trading Post Catalog of Arts & Crafts Supplies	$4.00